THE

PHILOSOPHY of FASCISM

By

MARIO PALMIERI

CHICAGO
THE DANTE ALIGHIERI SOCIETY
1936

FIRST EDITION

TO THE YOUTH OF AMERICA
THIS BOOK
POINTING THE WAY TO THE
DAWNING RENAISSANCE

PREFACE

In Italy, as well as abroad, much has been written about Fascism and its origin; so much indeed that the bibliography of Fascism is richer than that on any related subject.

And yet, notwithstanding all which has been written, very few, especially abroad, have understood its essence; and the true spiritual forces which generated it have not always received the right interpretation.

This work of Mr. Palmieri on "The Philosophy of Fascism" fills a greatly felt deficiency of such bibliography with its exposition of the spiritual aspects of Fascism, and is therefore highly appreciated in times like the present, when the desire to know Fascism in its true essence is becoming so thoroughly widespread.

It is thus on account of its unique worth that the "Philosophy of Fascism" appears under the aegis of the "Dante Alighieri National Society," magnificent herald of the Italian spirit in the world.

But Mr. Palmieri's work is not only honored by the seal of the "Dante" organization, but also by the approval of the father of Fascism, the Duce himself, his Excellency Benito Mussolini.

It is Mussolini who, with clear and far-seeing

vision of true Reality, has drawn the pattern of a new and higher form of social life founded upon the basis of a fairer and more rational distribution of the good things of life among the various classes of society.

Through the new Fascist conception and application of the Corporate State such re-distribution is taking place in Italy, and may in time take place elsewhere. Because if it is true that Fascism as a political system is something which cannot be exported, it is nevertheless also true that what constitutes the fundamental principles of its doctrine will always find useful application in modern societies.

Labor as duty for all, as a fundamental obligation toward the Nation-State, which is above everything and everybody, constitutes a conception of such importance that once realized in practice, it will not fail to bring about a more satisfactory form of social life.

It may thus very well happen that with the passing of time new countries may abandon the individualist way for this new way of life, in the hope that it may give them the possibility of further progress and further development within the boundaries of Order, Authority and Law.

I am therefore highly pleased that my trip to America has given me the opportunity of prefacing this book for its American edition, knowing that the American public will give it the support which it rightly deserves.

Dr. Guido Corni.

Member of Italian Parliament,
Honorary Governor of Somaliland.

Chicago, July 27, 1936.

CONTENTS

INTRODUCTION

THE Philosophy of Fascism! With the meaning of these very words, which may sound as a challenge to all ordinary ways of thinking about Fascism, is this book concerned.

Much has been written about and much more has been said of this dazzling social phenomenon of modern times which is called Fascism.

But whatever has been written or has been said has not touched as yet the core of the subject. The truth of it, that is the philosophy of it—as the historian of "The Rise of American Civilization" would be inclined to say—has not been expounded, or even questioned; and we are today still unaware whether it is possible for mankind to detect the glimmer of some great truth behind and beyond the pyrotechnic display of sensational events which have characterized the rise of Fascism.

The birth of the seventeenth year of Fascism as a theory of government and a doctrine of social organization, and the fourteenth year of Fascism as a political and social system in practical actuation, has been celebrated and hailed as conclusive, pragmatic proof that Fascism, both as a theory and as a fact, has established its claims to an unchallenged primacy in the realm of politics and in the world of action.

But a question has been raised of late, a question of paramount importance to every thinking man: namely, is there a coherent system of thought as foundation of Fascism? That is, granting all the claims of Fascism in the world of action, are its claims to unchallenged primacy in the world of thought as well justified by the existence of a philosophy of Fascism?

And the question cannot be lightly dismissed because Man is first of all and above all a spiritual being and, as such, wont to measure the ultimate worth of things according to a scale of intangible spiritual values, which has no place, for instance, for the so often hailed performance of running all the trains of Italy on perfect schedule, or for the transformation of malaria-infested swamps into real estate subdivisions.

He who thinks of Fascism and its worth thinks, primarily and above all, of what Fascism stands for in the realm of the spirit; of its contribution to man's spiritual heritage.

And unless Fascism is the material expression of a system of thought, the tranformation into reality of a body of ideas and a set of beliefs; the practical actuation, in a word, of a whole philosophy of life; unless Fascism is that, it cannot advance any claim to a complete primacy in the world of man.

Furthermore, a social and political system which affects the life of forty million people is bound, whether we are willing to admit it or not, to influence the ultimate destiny of the whole race of man.

It is, therefore, not only timely, but supremely necessary that the claims of Fascism to absolute pre-eminence in the realms of thought and action be set forth so that the world may be made aware of them and may examine them dispassionately; because it is the hope of Fascism that its worth may be proved or disproved only according to the light of reason and never according to the sway of irrational feelings and hysterical emotions.

This book represents, at the same time, an attempt to organize in a systematic exposition, those few fundamental original ideas which may truly deserve the right of forming part of The Philosophy of Fascism, and an attempt to determine the extent to which Fascism may influence the destinies of mankind, through the always wider diffusion and application of its principles; social, political, economic, etc.

Whether the book succeeds or not in fulfilling its ambitious task, and whether the Fascist philosophy of life is to remain as a permanent part of the intellectual and spiritual heritage of mankind, or is to be ultimately rejected and forgotten; it still remains true that Fascism is in this world with us at present; that it is a force we must reckon with, and that with its belief in the possibility of a world-wide spiritual renaissance, it holds for all people a message of deep significance, of universal application and of everlasting value.

MARIO PALMIERI.

"*Ideas rule the world and its events. A revolution is the passage of an Idea from theory to practice. Whatever men may say, material interests never have caused, and never will cause, a revolution. . . . Revolutions have their origin in the mind, in the very root of life; not in the material organism. . . . A religion or a philosophy lies at the base of every revolution. This is a truth that can be proved from the whole historical tradition of humanity.*"

—MAZZINI.

PART ONE
FASCISM AS A WAY OF LIFE

CHAPTER I

INDIVIDUALISM AND FASCISM

ONE invisible tie binds together the destinies
of all men. There cannot be any joy or any pain
experienced by one single individual, any good or
any evil befallen him, which shall not ultimately
affect the welfare of the race, the progress of the
world, the very course of history.

As the fall of a stone in a quiet pool draws at
the surface of the water concentric circles which
grow always wider in diameter until they extend
to the extreme limits of the pool, thus the consequences of a human deed which seemed at first
to affect the life of one man, grow little by little
to affect the lives of all men.

This recognition of the essential unity which is at
the very root of human life is part of that patrimony of eternally abiding truths which give meaning and purpose to that same life and constitute
the motive power of the actions of men.

But like the alternate ebb and flow of a cosmic
tide, obeying a mysterious law of cycles whose rhy-

thm is beyond our power to detect or control, alternate periods of time come into the light of this particular truth or recede from it, making of human history an ever changing tale of triumphs of the social instinct or of disintegrating effects of individualistic wills.

Looking at the kaleidoscopic succession of cultures, at the haphazard progress of mankind, at the rise and fall of civilizations, man has always asked whether it is possible to detect and trace the hidden thread which conects the apparently disconnected events; whether it is possible to discover any form of plan underlying the diversified variety of historical experience; whether, in short, it is possible at all to have a true philosophy of history.

And his answer to such a query has taken at different times different aspects, until, finally, the large number of proposed systems and explanations has convinced him that there is not one philosophy of history, but many, all equally true, and all equally valid, because all reflecting some Idea informing and giving light to the life of mankind. The systems of Vico, Schlegel, Herder, Marx, Hegel, all testify of this truth.

It is possible, therefore, and justified, to look at history as an alternate play of individualistic and anti-individualistic forces integrating and disintegrating in turn the social structure, the economic organization, the political systems, and all the other outward aspects of the life of man.

In the light of this particular form of philosophy of history whole periods of human affairs, deemed by common consent to be unusual, brilliant examples of the possibilities inherent to human nature, lose their brilliancy and their appeal and stand to testify of the innumerable pitfalls which beset the life of the spirit.

No other period of human history is deemed, in fact, to be more unique, more brilliant, than the period of the Renaissance. If ever man seemed to have found the true measure of his powers, it was then, when life was all one glory of artistic expression.

But the Renaissance sang not only the paean of Art, it sang also the birth of Individualism; the philosophy of life which was to guide, through the following centuries, the thoughts and the actions of men toward the present state of chaos and despair.

The invisible and imponderable forces which moulded the aspects assumed by the various manifestations of life of modern times were indeed born with the Renaissance; and the historian who attempts to portray the debacle of Individualism and the rise of Fascism must go back in time to discover the roots of this phenomenon within the fertile soil of ideas, theories, systems, etc., characterizing those eventful years.

It may seem, perhaps, somewhat far fetched to say that the rise of Fascism brings to a close a period of human history beginning as far back in time as the Renaissance. It is enough, nevertheless, to sound the hidden depths of meaning of the historical process to remain convinced of the soundness of the statement.

The Renaissance is commonly held to have been, and undoubtedly it was in a way, all that the name implies of re-birth of classical studies and pagan lore. Still, had it been only that and nothing else, had it meant for the world simply an artificial reproduction of old ideas, feelings, ways of living, etc., the Renaissance would have failed to represent a milestone in the road of human development. The spirit of the age had no true organic connection with the spirit of ancient times, and the classic-pagan-edonistic attitude of mankind throughout that age was at best a poor reproduction of something which represented a moment of human history forming part of the past, a past as dead as the men who of this moment were the brightest lights.

The Renaissance has importance, instead, inasmuch as it represents the birth of Individualism; the birth of a philosophy of life which was to hold sway over the thoughts and the actions of men for well nigh four centuries; those momentous centuries characterized by the greatest changes in all fields of human activity.

The birth of Individualism meant belief in man and his powers, hence the Reformation, which relying especially on man's reasoning power, transformed this belief into practical and, in a way, logical actuation with the doctrine of freedom from all authoritative rules of faith.

The birth of Individualism meant also the birth of freedom from all external authority, all external constraint, all external rules and laws; hence Liberalism which, forgetting that man is truly man only because he is part of a greater whole, proclaimed the doctrine of liberty, which is at the bottom only a doctrine of negative liberty.

The birth of Individualism meant in time a return to nature, hence the doctrine of his natural rights in politics, the doctrine of his material essence in philosophy, the doctrine of class war in economics, the negation of moral values in ethics.

The birth of Individualism meant in short the decay of all ties which connect man to the spiritual world and make of him a being thoroughly distinct from the world of nature.

It is thus that if the Renaissance is to be rightly understood, the ominous significance and the evil influence of Individualism must need be made part of, and integrated within, that complex picture filled by the birth of experimental science, the re-birth of art, and the revival of classical studies.

What is Individualism, then?

Individualism is the negation of the fundamental unity which is at the root of Being and which underlies the whole world of man; is the negation of the principle of Authority which re-attaches, through intermediate stages, the fleeting individual to the eternal source of justice and power; is the negation of that principle of Liberty which can be truly worthy of its name when it releases man of the tyranny of his needs, his desires and his wants, and makes him choose—of his own free will—what is of higher value than the satisfaction of the senses; is the negation of the principle of Duty which is the foundation of the moral world and the affirmation in its stead of the principle of Rights—those rights which are the perennial spring of all human ills and evils; is the negation of the spiritual essence of man and the affirmation that what is paramount for man is his material, economic, or bodily well being and that this welfare is worth any other being's suffering, disgrace or death; is the glorification of each individual as center and lord of the whole universe and the apotheosis, consequently, of his individual needs, passions and desires; is, finally, the triumph of the reasoning faculties of the mind over the mystic powers of the soul.

It is thus that, guided by the tenets of such a fatal philosophy of life, man was no longer concerned with the great beyond, with the ideals of ethics, with the triumph of law and justice, with the dream of salvation, with visions of great feats of the spirit.

With the advent of modern times man became primarily and above all concerned with his own welfare and, since belief in the soul was finally destroyed by the misinterpreted findings of science, this welfare meant in the end only and simply the welfare of his own body.

The search for a meaning of life ended at the same time with the discovery that the individual is the center of the whole universe and that this universe is nothing more than a play-field ready at hand for the expression of his personality.

Individualism asserting itself and triumphing thus above every other conception of life, gradually led mankind through democratic government, competitive business, acquisitive property, hereditary wealth, economic individual warfare, social class struggle and national wars, to a state of things of which it is already possible to visualize the outcome—that outcome prophesied so clearly and so forcefully by Oswald Spengler in "The Decline of the West."

Looked at, therefore, in the light of the pernicious influence exercised by the philosophy of life to which itgave birth, the Renaissance loses most of its glamorous appeal and remains to signify, in the word of Gentile:

"The age of Individualism which led the people, through the splendid dreams of art and poetry to the indifference, the skepticism and the sordid slothfulness of men who have nothing to defend outside of themselves, neither in the family nor in the fatherland, nor in the wide world where every human personality, conscious of its own worth and its own dignity, has its true roots. This is because the individual believed in nothing which could transcend the carefree, happy play of his own creative fancy. . . . Man, become suddenly conscious of his greatness, asks for liberty; and, as a particular individual, he deems himself entitled to that infinite worth which only belongs to the life of the spirit."

The Renaissance had its day of glory and then, as all mortal things, it became a thing of the past; but man, drunk with his newly discovered freedom, driven onward by his instincts and his physiological needs, carried on the daily business of living more and more relentlessly, ruthlessly, trampling over the bodies and the souls of his less endowed, less powerful fellow beings; satisfied with the existing order of things, fashioning for himself materialistic, positivistic, pragmatistic theories, to explain facts as he desires them to be explained.

It is only of late that a grievous sense of the futility of all human efforts and a torturing doubt

about the validity of Individualism as the true answer to the problems of life, began to cast their
ominous shadow across the whole breadth of the
western world.

A whole realm of values which man had set for
himself as things of supreme worth, and for the
realization of which he was ready to struggle and
suffer, has lost gradually the support of his faith
and has been engulfed in that sea of pessimism and
despair which is submerging the very life of mankind.

The question must be raised then—and it is supremely timely that it be raised now—whether
Individualism represents the true answer to the
quest of man for the right philosophy of life.

It is in the very nature of man, in fact, that he
cannot remain long satisfied with the assumption
that the life of the spirit is ended with a concern
for the individual's bodily welfare, and that for
him there is therefore nothing else left than to eat
and drink and beget other children who, in turn,
shall eat and drink and have children, so that the
repetition of this seemingly perpetual cycle of birth,
life, death and re-birth, may never come to an end.

And because he cannot remain satisfied with that
assumption, every system of individual and social
life based upon the truth of the fundamental ani-
mality of man is inevitably doomed to failure.

Such a system can only stress the claims of the
individual to complete self-expression and make of
these claim the highest goal and the true end of life.
But the claims of one individual must need conflict
with the claims of another; the life of one being
must needs be at war with the life of the whole if

those claims are to be triumph; an effort must be made to break the invisible tie which binds together the destinies of all men, if the life of the one be set against the life of another; a whole endless series of evils arises in short whenever and wherever Individualism triumphs as a philosophy and a way of life.

It is thus clearly seen that the conditions which made possible the rise of Fascism arose from the basic conceptions on which the modern life of the western world is based. These conditions are not peculiar to one nation, but to all nations.

It is the current materialistic, mechanistic, individualistic conception of life, with its negation of the spiritual essence of man and with its assumption of a godless universe in which man is subject to only one rule: the rule of his animal nature, that has prepared the soil for the rise of Fascism.

It is the apparent debacle of all human efforts for a better life, the apparent impossibility to bring about some form of order out of the present state of chaos and stop the prophesied downfall of western civilization; it is the realization that man, left free to gratify his lust of power, his greed of gold, his love of the senses, his worship of force, is a pitiful and despicable being; and it is, finally, the vision that a higher calling must be the true heritage of man, that has brought about the birth of Fascism.

It is the fact that man has lost faith in himself, the fact that he cannot derive any support from his inner world and that he finds himself compelled to grope for aid in the outer world; it is the acknowledged fact of his sad moral decadence, in short, that has made possible the triumph of Fascism.

And, finally, it is the growing complexity of human relationships in all fields: the social as well as the moral, the economic as well as the spiritual, and the growing dependency of the single individual upon his fellow beings and upon society as a whole, that constitute the reason of being of Fascism.

Nothing could be more fallacious, therefore, than the general conviction that the historical process which made possible the development of Fascism and was, in a way, the primary condition of its birth, is a purely localized experience of one nation: the Italian nation. The conditions out of which Fascism arose were, and still are, conditions affecting the whole civilized world; conditions which perpetuated in time, must need create an increasing demand for the generalized application of the universal principles of Fascism.

If it is true that "Historia magistra vitae," then the lesson which history teaches must also be true: the lesson, namely, that the experience of life of the western world is a unified experience, that any local development is bound to affect this western world in all its parts, and that the whole structure of western civilization is bound to stand or fall together.

It is thus that if in its immediate manifestations of new social system, new form of political and economic organization, and new theory of government, Fascism appears to be a product of its times and of that particular country in which it had its birth; in its transcendent expression—that expression of a phenomenon of the activity of the spirit which alone is of ultimate value—Fascism is beyond the limitations of time and space; its roots are in the depths of Being, its flowers in the realm of Becoming.

These two forms of Fascism: the superficial aspect of its immediate manifestations and the deeper aspect of its ultimate expression correspond in a way to the current notion which the world at large holds about Fascism, and to the inner knowledge gained by those who have concerned themselves with the discovery of the idea behind the fact, of the truth below the artifice, of the reality beyond the appearance.

It is not unusual to hear, in fact, that Fascism is merely a change of the social and political system of one nation, or the revolt of the middle class, or the organization of the capitalistic groups, or the domination of the militaristic caste; also the tool of despotism, the product of reaction, the creature of dictatorship, the instrument of brutal, incontinent violence, and, finally, the nemesis of liberty.

But all these definitions fail to seize the central truth of Fascism. They place in distorted relief some of the transitory aspects of the phenomenon, but shed no light upon its permanent and universal elements, that is, upon that inner core of Fascism which only has meaning and value for the whole world of men.

Fascism is something more, something infinitely greater than a tyrannical dictatorship over the souls and the bodies of men, something of deeper import than a new form of economic organization, or a mere change of the social and political system of one nation.

What is Fascism, then?

This is the question of all questions: What is Fascism?

Fascism is an eminently idealistic and, more specifically, an anti-materialistc and anti-individualistic philosophy of life. These characteristics are clearly expressed by the recognition of the eternal value of the spiritual essence of man and of the transitory aspect of his earthly being; by the recognition of the absolute worth of the individual in the realm of the Spirit and of the relative worth of the individual in the realm of Nature; by the recognition of the transcendent significance of the historical process and of the fundamental continuity of human history; by the recognition of the supreme role played in the life of mankind by those social formations called Family and Nation, and of the small importance of the role played by the single individual; by the recognition of the influence of Religion on human life, and of the supremacy in this life of Ethics over Economics, of Art over Business, of Poetry over Science, of Intuition and Inspiration over Experience and Method; by the recognition of the supremely ethical nature of the State, and of the function of the State as concrete expression in the realm of time and space of the timeless idea of the nation; by the recognition of the truth that mankind needs an aristocracy of leaders led, in turn, by national heroes; of the need that the doctrine of the Duties of Man be substituted to the doctrine of the Rights of Man; of the fact that Man lives not by bread alone but also, and mainly, of beliefs; and, finally, of the truth that all forms of personal freedom pale in contrast to that form of Liberty which only has meaning and truly matters: the Liberty of the Spirit.

Fascism turns toward the individual to tell him:

Thy life has no absolute, no eternal value whatsoever; thy life can assume worth only inasmuch as it is devoted and, if necessary, sacrificed to the triumph of an Idea. Men live today, die tomorrow, but Ideas live forever. And the one who will seek to save his own life shall truly lose it, because only by offering it in holocaust to an everlasting Idea does individual life partake of the character of immortality.

This meaning of life as triumph of a remote ideal over the immediate reality, of the universal over the individual, is the fundamental characteristic of Fascism. But the creed of the worthlessness of human life when concerned simply with the material welfare of man is not a new one in the history of human thought. All through the ages great leaders and seers have sounded a warning for mankind to heed; a warning left, alas! always unheeded by the masses. The last prophetic voice heard on the shores of America was that of Emerson who, speaking before the Senior Class in Divinity College at Cambridge on a Sunday evening of July, 1838, said:

"Life is comic or pitiful as soon as the high ends of being fade out of sight and a man becomes nearsighted and can only attend to what addresses the senses."

But Emerson has been long dead and his message sounds strangely alien in twentieth century America.

The Idea Fascism — that is, Emerson's very thought carried to its logical conclusion—is in the process of being transformed instead, by a strange turn of fate, into living reality by another nation.

The search for a meaning of life is ended thus, for that nation, with the realization that what must be paramount for man is not the conception of his rights as individual but the vision of his duties as social being, that what is of supreme worth is not personal life but the life of the nation; and that, finally, human life is at bottom not a gratification of the senses but an expression of the soul and, as such, not a vehicle of happiness, but a bearer of sorrow, because only through sorrow does the soul learn, as Novalis said,

". . . those things which partake of the truth and outlast the centuries."

Fascism sounding anew the call to an ascetic and heroic view of life must then be thought of as a spiritual principle, or, rather, as a coherent and unified body of spiritual principles.

The very fact that Fascism has been able to furnish the modern world with a new meaning for life, and, consequently, with a new reason for living, struggling, suffering and dying, requires that something of transcendent significance must lie at the root, and constitute the true essence, of Fascism

But also the birth of Fascism, its growth, its development and progress testify of the fact that it is not a by-product of material circumstances, but a phenomenon of the spiritual world which originated from the creative element in man, and which can create, in turn, new and never dreamed-of material conditions.

Nothing has contributed so effectively to the general misunderstanding of Fascism as the ignorance of such a fundamental truth. And nothing will serve so effectively to awaken mankind to the realization of its plight as the vision and the knowledge of the true role of Fascism. It will happen thus that, as more time will pass, it will appear always more clearly and more forcefully evident that all which was thought so far to constitute the essence of Fascism: dictatorship, imperialism, nationalism, militarism, etc., represent nothing more than external accretions upon the inner core which falls under the domain of human history. Human history, that is, thought of not as a disconnected series of unrelated events, but as the progressive development of Ideas in one organic, unbroken process.

At bottom the fifteenth century, the sixteenth, the eighteenth and so forth, are, in fact, nothing more than the Renaissance, the Reform, the Enlightenment; that is the very Ideas which impressed their mark upon them.

In the same way it is true that the twentieth century will undoubtedly pass to history as the age of the Fascist Renaissance whether we choose to accept it or not, because some of the greatest spiritual principles ruling the world of action of today are the principles of Fascism.

But the esoteric aspect of Fascism is not exhausted by its entirely original solution of that eternal riddle: the meaning of life. There is, in fact, another equally tormenting problem left still without adequate solution, although it is generally agreed that the finding of the right solution is of paramount importance for mankind. That problem can be stated briefly thus: "What is the good life? And how can mankind ever rise to the vision and the realization of the good life? In other words, what should the conduct of life be?"

In the end all improvements of the social, political and economic organization of mankind cannot be considered to be anything else but better means of bringing about a more adequate realization of the life of the spirit in the world of man.

At no time then must these improvements be mistaken for the end and the goal of life; that goal is not to build better houses, wider roads, finer schools; is not to create more wealth and to distribute it equally; is not to increase well-being and happiness; the goal of life is the spiritualization of man. But how can it ever be reached? What is the path to the good life? Questions of this type are of tragic import and must receive some form of answer if human life is to be truly human at all.

We find thus that it is especially in its effort to make the conduct of life dependent from the practical application of great spiritual principles that Fascism seems to answer to the need of the hour.

The conduct of life must rest upon three great unalterable principles, Fascism maintains; namely, the principle of Unity, the principle of Authority, and the principle of Duty. They are the basis of Society, the foundation of Law and the essence of the moral order. Upon them it is possible to raise the edifice of a stable human life ruled by Justice and inspired by Ethics. Without them there cannot be anything else but anarchy, wantonness and chaos.

In stating these cardinal principles of the conduct of life, Fascism becomes invested with dignity and power and worth, and conquers anew the right to the deeper interpretation of its doctrine as a comprehensive philosophy of life; nay, as a veritable WAY OF LIFE, a way of life which entails the triumph of the soul over greed and fear; greed of lust, of power, of gold; fear of poverty, of disgrace, sufferance, martyrdom and death.

> Man does not live by bread alone but also, and mainly, of beliefs. Given an inspiring set of beliefs man may be able to accomplish great deeds and the world may be vivified by a new age of faith.

This is the first article of the Fascist creed, and the one to which that magnificent germination of spiritual energies we are witnessing today in the land of Italy owes mainly its birth.

It is with such an article of faith that Fascism has struck a decisive blow at the root of the evil undermining the structure of western civilization, and sapping the very vitality of the modern world. This mortal evil is not the machine; it is not over-population; it is not concentration of wealth. No, it is simply the lack of a common faith which alone can make of mankind one living unity and bring man at last to forsake the individualistic claims of the ego for the good of the whole.

Man does not live by bread alone. . . .

It is not Fascism which has discovered this truth

lying at the very basis of life itself, but it is Fascism which has transformed it, for the first time in the history of mankind, into living reality in the life of a whole nation. It is Fascism which has brought mankind to face and to acknowledge once more the fundamental fact of life: the fact that—in the words of Carlyle—

> ". . . the thing a man does practically lay at heart and know for certain concerning his vital relation to this mysterious universe, and his duty and destiny there, that is in all cases the primary thing for him and creatively determines all the rest."

Since the day of its birth Fascism recognized the need of restoring the faith of mankind in a set of beliefs capable to vivify the present unbelieving, unsatisfactory and aimless life into a new expression of power, of energy, of achievements.

It is thus on account of this recognition of mankind's deepest need and of the vision and realization of a better life that Fascism deserves to be hailed as the herald of a new age: the age which will witness the triumph of the whole realm of spiritual values over the petty and selfish aims of the individual ego.

Man does not live by bread alone. . . .

How strange that at each decisive turn of human history man should be reminded anew of this truth which is the very foundation of life.

Given an inspiring set of beliefs man may be able to accomplish great deeds and the world may be vivified by a new age of faith. Among all beliefs paramount must always be held the belief in the spiritual essence of man. It is only such a belief, Fascism maintains, that can bring the individual to value the things of supreme import: the welfare of the nation, the progress of the race, the growth of knowledge, the liberation of the spirit within.

It is this belief of Fascism in the essential spirituality of the nature of man; it is its recognition of the invisible tie which binds together the destinies of all mortal beings; it is its faith in a world of values of far greater import than the values of the sensual life; it is its call to a regeneration of the race and to the amalgamation of the people of each country into a living unity; it is its purpose to make of the State—that is of the highest form of political organization known to man—the visible, tangible expression of the nation; it is its aim to set the welfare of the State above the welfare of the individual, to make of the enrichment of the life of the nation the motive power of the life of the citizen; and it is, finally, its ambition to place ideals above wants, sacrifices above desires, heroism, martyrdom and death above cowardice, safety and well-being, what definitely and resolutely sets Fascism as the antithesis and the nemesis of Individualism.

"To be rightly understood, the Fascist movement must be considered in all its breadth and depth of spiritual phenomenon. Fascism is in fact a spiritual revolt against those ideologies which corrupted the sacred principles of Religion, Fatherland and Family. Fascism may not show in its true aspects in the single individual and in social groups, but in its purest expression the flame of Fascism is immortal because it is the very flame of the Spirit. And if it is true that matter has been enshrined on our altars during a whole century, it is also true that it is the Spirit which today will take its place."

These words of the father of Fascism represent the key to the right comprehension of the significance and the importance of this characteristic product of our own era. Because if Fascism in its purest expression is truly a thing of the Spirit, if beyond and behind the surface appearance of local phenomenon it enjoys an esoteric interpretation of transcendent significance for the whole of mankind, if it can be considered not as an outward display of sensational aspects, but as an inward message of new philosophy of life—that philosophy of life that is to take the place of our glorified and, nevertheless, so poignantly unsatisfactory because so brutally destructive, Individualism—it is then still possible that the prophesied "Decline of the West" may be definitely halted and, in its stead, we may witness the birth of a new and greater Renaissance.

"The life of Man is more than animal life; it is also, and mainly, the life of the Spirit." —TOLSTOI.

CHAPTER II

FASCIST IDEALISM AND MODERN MATERIALISM

MAN is above, outside, and against Nature.

Man is part and product of Nature.

These two visions of man, like the two poles of Being, set in antithesis to each other and separated by an unabridgeable chasm, represent the keys to the right understanding of these two contrasting philosophies of our times: Fascist Idealism and modern Materialism.

The moment that we think of man as a being gifted with the gifts of the Spirit, and, therefore, endowed with the power of creation, with the ability to transcend the contingencies of his material life, with the desire to rise above the determinism of outward events and inward needs, with the aspiration toward a life which is not of this earth but belongs to the magic land of his beliefs and his dreams; that moment marks also our entrance in the realm of Fascist Idealism.

41

The moment, instead, that we think of man bound to the world of nature, unable to free himself from the shackles and the fetters of his sense experiences, an animal among animals—the only difference between his life and their life being his peculiar subjection to the action of mysterious laws of economics which can make of the existence of the greater number of his brethren a veritable hell on earth—that moment marks also our acquaintance with Materialism, the philosophical doctrine characterizing the way of life of so large a part of the modern world.

Materialism, to be sure, is not a product of our age. As a stream underlying the verdant expanse of green meadows and opulent pastures which, from time to time, comes to the surface of the earth, to disappear again, engulfed in a subterranean course, thus materialism—or its equivalents: naturalism and realism—has, since the beginnings of history, risen from time to time to the surface of man's conscious life and shaped the type of his reaction to his environment and to the life of his fellow beings.

This is because entrenched in the deepest recesses of his own nature man harbors within himself the primitive instincts of all animal beings. Ever recurring waves of spiritual exaltation force these instincts into the background of his conscious life, but the moment the wave subsides, the moment the voice within grows dull and inarticulate, those instincts come readily and invariably to the fore to assert themselves over and against the creations of the spirit.

Thus it happened that the rise of Christianity

destroyed what will remain perhaps the crassest form of materialism the world has ever known only to make room in time for a newer and subtler one. Thus it happened that the resplendent vision of the Kingdom of God which had brightened for a while the horizon of man's life, inspired his thoughts, moved his heart, lost gradually its lustre and faded finally into a blurred and distorted image.

Thus it happened that the certainty of a better life changed slowly in the memory of a promise which was never fulfilled and was never to be, perhaps, fulfilled.

Thus it happened, finally, that the ground was prepared for the rise of modern materialism, born with the birth of science, grown lusty with the growth of the machine, and become in the end a veritable religion with man's fashioning of such idols for his worship as Wealth, Comfort, Success and Progress.

And, yet, there has never been a more forceful appeal made to the best in man than the appeal made by Christianity. The Idealism born of it, and constituting in a way its main characteristic feature, spoke always directly to the Soul and through the Soul. It spoke of a world of values which were not of this earth and which far transcended everything which the earth could offer. It spoke of another life, more alluring than the present earthly one, a life unseen by mortal eyes, but, nevertheless, far more vivid than any other thing perceived. It spoke, finally, of the existence of another form of reality, unknown to man in his ordinary state, but of which he could get fleeting glimpses in his rare moments of mystic consciousness; and, speaking of this reality as the only reality, it denounced the one apprehended by the mind through the intermediary of the experience of senses, as a most illusory and deceiving one.

Such was, and, for that matter, still is, the message delivered by the religious Idealism born of Christianity.

Of such message man lived once; in such message man believed once. Alas! how those times and that belief are part of the past. To modern man the present and earthly life is the only life he is interested in. Such undreamed-of realms of action are offered to his eyes; such never dreamed-of opportunities for work, achievements, discoveries, inventions, has science placed at his disposal; so many are his tools and his goals, that modern man believes—rightly or wrongly—that all his energy, all his power, all his ambition, must be devoted, and cannot fail to be devoted, to the life of the world of everyday experience, that world of which he feels to be integral part, and which holds such great and alluring promises to him.

The other world, the world of the Spirit, is become unspeakably remote and strange. The values which modern man prizes and covets are not invisible, spiritual values, but material and tangible ones. Did not recently the head of a great nation announce as supreme blessing for his people the presence of an automobile in every garage and a chicken in every pot? Time it was, instead, and not so far ago for mankind to have forgotten it already, when the leader of a nation would claim as supreme blessings for its people the fulfillment of such ideals as the respect of age, the love of all men, the pursuit of truth, the quest for beauty, the striving after perfection.

How can religious Idealism, in such a changed world, ever re-conquer the position it has lost: that position of pre-eminence in the direction of the affairs of men which has been usurped by the gods of materialism?

Clearly, there is no hope left; at least not for the present. Time will come, perhaps in a future much nearer that we would fain to believe, when Religion will re-acquire its hold upon the life of man. But for the present, let us be sincere to ourselves, Religion is a vacuous thing for modern man, and Religious Idealism a formula devoid of all meaning, all value, all attraction.

And, yet, modern man is not and cannot be satisfied with life in its present state.

Tragic, infinitely more tragic, in effect, than the debacle of our economic organization is that decay of a genuine life of the spirit evinced by the prevalent idolatry of our religious life, the sordid meanness of our social life, the vacuous futility of our intellectual life, and the sterile efforts of our artistic life.

Churches have multiplied, but not a new word of salvation issues out of them.

Universities have increased in number, but academic learning is stifling all spiritual activity.

Libraries are covering the land, but information has taken the place of erudition.

Knowledge is spreading, but of that unilateral, superficial, partial kind which is the most dangerous of all forms of knowledge.

Science, unable to approach the core of ultimate

45

reality, pretends nevertheless, to assume the role of arbiter of the life of man.

Intelligence and Method have taken the place of Intuition and Imagination.

No great Art is born. ". . . all belief is extinct, we have no faith in our gods, no belief in the Republic. Great principles are no more. Material interests reign supreme. The multitude demands bread and amusements."

Truly our times are strangely reminiscent of the days of decay of other forms of culture; once again, man, now engaged in an anxious, relentless quest after fuller and more satisfying experiences of the senses, may reach much sooner than he thinks the end of the road on which he has been traveling in these last three hundred years. Then, when he will be forced to turn back and face the test of what constitute the supreme realities of his life and his world, what can be offered to him as an anchorage for his inner life, that life which he may repudiate, but which he can never deny?

It is, thus, in times like the present when everything points to destruction and chaos, when the feared "Decline of the West" seems more than ever an inevitable possibility, when the support of Religion is vanished and the tenets of a religious Idealism are totally in disrepute, that a new form of Idealism is bound to arise to deliver a new message of hope for mankind and re-shape not only the course, but the very basis of human life.

It is in times like the present when man's only happiness is found in sensuous enjoyment alone, when man's religious life is become a perfunctory performance of ritualistic and meaningless practices, when the life of the spirit is at its lowest ebb, that there is high need for a new revival of Idealism as a philosophy and a way of life.

What shall the aspects of this new Idealism be? It cannot, evidently, be a re-affirmation of old theories and old principles. Neither can it be an academic discussion of abstract systems of beliefs without relation to the world of facts. To be a vital force in the life of modern man, the new Idealism must above all deliver a message in tune with the needs of this life as it is being lived today, and not as it ought to be lived in a future which may never dawn. Furthermore, the new Idealism must of necessity take into account all the complexity of the modern world. To deny this complexity, or to ignore some aspects of this world, would spell beforehand the doom of any philosophic doctrine which attempts to interpret or direct the present state of affairs.

The whole realm of facts, experiences and values born with the birth of Science, must thus be brought within the higher synthesis of the new Idealism to a congruous, harmonious relationship with all other realms of man's life.

Finally, the new Idealism must not remain an intellectual pastime of the élite, but must leaven the life of the masses. It is to the masses and not to the few that the new Idealism must bring its message of salvation, and bring it in such a form as to make it easily intelligible and readily accepted— because salvation is not a privilege of the intellectuals, but a need of the people. That is, salvation, from what makes the people forgetful of the existence of something higher and nobler than the life

47

of the body, and leads them to exchange, for a belief in the abiding reality of things unseen, their belief in the illusory and deceptive transitoriness of the world of senses.

Above all, the message of the new Idealism must be a message for the man of today: the man whom we all know; one of us, our brother, brother in spirit if not in flesh, with our vices and our virtues, our hopes and our failures, our sorrows and our joys, our aspirations and our dreams.

Only in this way can the new Idealism conquer a place in our mind and in our heart, change our whole way of life, and thus bring about our own salvation.

Such must the distinguishing features of the new Idealism be; such indeed are the distinguishing features of Fascist Idealism.

To comprehend them in detail it is enough to become acquainted with their abridged form in the brief but masterly exposition of the principles of Fascism by Mussolini himself.

". . . Fascism is action and is thought: action in which doctrine is immanent, and doctrine arising from a given system of historical forces in which it is inserted and working on them from within. It has therefore a form correlated to contingencies of time and space; but it has also an ideal content which makes it an expression of truth in the higher regions of the history of thought. There is no possibility of exercising a spiritual influence in the world as a human will dominating the will of others, unless one has a conception both of the transient and the specific reality on which that action is to be exercised, and of the permanent and universal reality in which the transient dwells and has its being.

"To know men one must know man: and to know man one must be acquainted with reality and its laws. There can be no conception of the State which is not fundamentally a conception of life: it may be philosophy or intuition, or system of ideas evolving within the framework of logic or concentrated in a vision or a faith, but it is always, at least potentially, an organic conception of the world.

"Thus many of the practical expressions of Fascism—such as party organization, system of education, dicipline—can be understood only when considered in relation to its general attitude toward life; a truly spiritual attitude. Fascism sees in the world not only those superficial, material aspects in which man appears as an individual, standing by himself, self-centered, subject to natural law which instinctively urges him toward a life of selfish momentary pleasure; it sees not only the individual but the nation and the country; individuals and generations bound together by a moral law, with common traditions and a mission which, suppressing the instinct for life confined in a brief cycle of pleasure, builds up a higher life, founded on duty, a life free from the limitations of time and space, in which the individual, by self-sacrifice, the renunciation of self-interest, by death itself, can achieve that purely spiritual existence in which his value as a man consists.

"The conception is therefore a spiritual one, arising from the general reaction of the century against the flaccid materialistic positivism of the nineteenth century. Anti-positivistic but positive; neither skeptical nor agnostic; neither pessimistic nor supinely optimistic as are, generally speaking, the doctrines (all negative), which place the center of life outside man; whereas, by the exercise of his free will, man can and must create his own world.

"Fascism wants man to be active and to engage in action with all his energies; it wants him to be manfully aware of the difficulties besetting him and ready to face them. It conceives of life as a struggle in which it behooves a man to win for himself a really worthy place, first of all by fitting himself (physically, morally, intellectually) to become the implement required for winning it. As for the individual, so for the nation, and so for mankind. Hence the high value of culture in all of its forms (artistic, religious, scientific) and the outstanding importance of education. Hence also the essential value of work, by which man subjugates nature and creates the human world (economic, political, ethical, intellectual).

"This positive conception of life is obviously an ethical one. It invests the whole field of reality as well as the human activities which master it. No action is exempt from moral judgment; no activity can be despoiled of the value which a moral purpose confers on all things. Therefore life, as conceived of by the Fascist, is serious, austere, religious; all its manifestations are poised in a world sustained by moral forces and subject to spiritual responsibilities. The Fascist disdains an "easy" life.

"The Fascist conception of life is a religious one in which man is viewed in his immanent relation to a higher law, endowed with an objective will transcending the individual and raising him to conscious membership of a spiritual society.

"In the Fascist conception of history, man is man only by virtue of the spiritual process to which he contributes as a member of the family, the social group, the nation, and of the history to which all nations bring their contribution. Hence the great value of tradition in records, in language, in customs, in the rules of social life. Outside history man is a nonentity.

"Fascism is therefore opposed to all individualistic abstractions based on eighteenth century materialism; and it is opposed to all Jacobinistic utopias and innovations. It does not believe in the possibility of happiness on earth as conceived by the economistic literature of the eighteenth century, and it therefore rejects the teleological notion that at some future time the human family will secure a final settlement of all its difficulties. This notion runs counter to experience which teaches that life is in continual flux and in process of evolution.

"In politics Fascism aims at realism; in practice it desires to deal only with those problems which are the spontaneous products of historic conditions and which find or suggest their own solutions. Only by entering within the process of reality and taking possession of the forces at work in it, can man ever act on man and on nature."

Such is the "Manifesto" of Fascist Idealism.

Such is the message of Fascism.

This message is a call: a call to the new life. Too long has the human spirit suffered the thralldom of Nature. Too long has man worshipped the false gods of material possessions. The new life, the Fascist way of life, shall be a new creation of the human spirit awakened at last to the full consciousness of its dignity.

Striking at the root of the evil which poisons the very springs of his being, Fascism tells Man that it is high time for him to set himself definitely above, outside and against Nature. Cutting abruptly the Gordian knot which keeps him a slave of his physiological needs and material hindrances, Fascism tells Man: "Arise, at last, come into thine own, reach the full stature of thy being, fulfill thy mission in the world, be the master of thine own destiny."

The Fascist way of life is thus life as it ought be lived: a life, that is, of devotion to those Ideals which form the very substance of the world of the Spirit, that world of timeless and absolute values which partakes of the essence of God and to which belongs the true essence of Man.

In the Fascist way of life man, become conscious at last, of his sense of responsibility toward his fellow beings, will transform the conception of the brotherhood of all human beings into a fact, the vision of the indissoluble tie which makes of their destinies one interrelated whole into a reality.

In the Fascist way of life there is no room for a social system which allows to a few privileged individuals the right to control the lives of one hundred millions or more of his fellow beings; for a social system which hides behind the gaudy trappings of apparently democratic political forms the most revolting form of economic slavery the masses have ever experienced, and which, denouncing, therefore, political tyranny, attempts and succeeds in imposing upon the people the worst tyranny of all: that of depriving them of their right to self-expression, their right to work, their right to bread.

In the Fascist way of life there is no room for a type of culture which is only an intellectual sport of the élite: true culture is for Fascism the spontaneous flowering of the spirit within when a whole nation is stirred by the vivifying call to a higher life, to a life of duty, sacrifice and heroism.

In the Fascist way of life there is no room for a type of civilization which has undermined the very foundations of all human progress—what took aeons of time to bring forth from the chaos of brutality and savagery and will remain the supreme achievements of man—namely, those institutions called the Church, the Family and the State.

In the Fascist way of life there is no Religion outside the Church, no Love outside the Family, no Liberty outside the State.

The realization of such a way of life requires that man become once more a believer in the reality of the unseen, requires that he assume again a humble attitude toward the unsolved mysteries of life and death, and birth and creation, requires that he experience again the power of the great forces of the Spirit.

Then, and only then, will he be ready for the new spring of his inner world, for the great awakening of his inner self, for the coming renaissance of the new life.

CHAPTER III

FASCISM AND THE MEANING OF LIFE

There is a question that man has always asked at every crucial time of his history, and that question is: "What is the meaning and purpose of this life of mine? Has it a mission to fulfill, a goal to reach, a plan to unfold? Or is it only and simply 'a tale full of fury, signifying nothing'?"

Spurred by the need of giving some kind of answer to a question which cannot be left unanswered, man has been forced then to examine critically the foundations, the course and the aspects of human life, to discover whether they give any hint of a transcendent meaning and a worthy goal.

It is thus that the Hindu seer found that life HAS a meaning and that this meaning consists of the identification of the individual consciousness with the consciousness of the Whole, and that the true goal of life is the Nirvana, that blessed state in which there is extinction of all which impedes the possibility of such identification.

The Greek thinker, instead, found the meaning

of life in a full and joyous dedication of all individual efforts to the furthering of an Ideal, and the goal of life in the harmonious development and ultimate perfection of all human faculties.

We see the Romans find this meaning in the worship of Law, of Order, of Justice, and their national life become fruitful and triumphant. We see them lose this meaning little by little, and the civilization they created become correspondingly sterile and finally decline.

The Christian Fathers, on the other hand, held that human life is but a preparation for a higher and nobler life to be lived not on this earth but in another world—a world of which we have no knowledge and the existence of which cannot be either proved or disproved—and that the goal of life is not the extinction of individuality or the perfection of personality, but salvation from our own selves and redemption of our own selves.

We see this vision of life illuminate a full cycle of human history and assist, awed and amazed, to the exultant raising of those mighty symphonies of stone which are the Gothic cathedrals.

We see the men of the Renaissance find this meaning in the triumph of the Spirit within and their life become one magnificent glory of spiritual expression.

Throughout the whole process of history we assist in other words, to the unfolding of powers and energies within man of almost divine nature, of almost god-like essence, whenever his anxious quest for meaning of life has led him to visualize and worship a deeper reality lying behind and beyond the immediate and closely bound world of his own self.

But with the advent of modern man the scene changes. Man is no longer concerned with the Ideals of Beauty, of Law, of Authority; is no longer interested in the life beyond; is no longer living for the triumph of the spirit within.

With the advent of modern times man is simply and solely concerned with his own welfare, and since this welfare means only the satisfaction of his bodily needs and desires, a thoroughly materialistic view of life which has no place for the worship of such intangible things as the worship of Ideals, triumphs over and against all which had been held great and dignified and worthy in human life.

It is thus that modern man, rejecting all other interpretations of the meaning of life as expressions of a dead and soon to be forgotten past, maintains that it is highly doubtful whether life has a meaning at all, and that, at best, this meaning consists only of the fullest realization of one's own possibilities, and that the goal of life is to bring about such a realization here on this earth and not in a hypothetical world which may never exist and at a future time which may never dawn.

In consistence with this view of life, modern man has waged a relentless war against all which appeared to him to place restrictions on his freedom, because only in unfettered freedom does he believe it possible to realize his Will to live.

He has consequently rejected all the claims of the Church upon his conduct of life, all the claims of the State upon his person and his goods, all the claims of the Family upon his time, his energies and his affections.

To suit his view of life he has demanded and obtained that the function of the Church be restricted to that of an institution of meaningless ritualistic practices, which may have been once the expression of some deep truths but are now simply forms without substance, trappings of a show from which all spirit has fled.

He has also demanded and obtained that the State become a creature of his will, whose main function must be that of an institution capable of protecting his life, his people and his property while interfering the least possible with his undertakings, his plans and his schemes.

Finally, he has demanded and obtained that the Family be changed from an institution of permanent relationships and binding ties, to an institution of transient character, which can be temporarily patronized, easily dissolved and lightly regarded.

To let all this come to pass he has made a slogan of the word Liberty, which has become for him a truly magic word capable of unlocking the doors of heaven on earth, and of offering him what he has always sought and has never found because it can never be found: viz; material and sensual happiness.

In the name of religious liberty he has undermined Religion, in the name of political liberty he has nullified the State, in the name of economic liberty he has enslaved his brethren, in the name of personal liberty he has destroyed the Family.

A thoroughly materialistic view of human life has thus brought about the triumph of the individual's animalistic will to live over the individual's spiritual aspirations, and the downfall of those institutions which took mankind aeons of time to bring into being and represent the true achievements of man on this earth.

Highly revealing are, consequently, the signs of the times. It is given to us to assist in effect to the spectacle, sad and amusing at the same time, of a man, who has never been able to transform a relationship of bodies into a communion of souls, change his wife for the third, fourth or fifth time, in the hope of reaching the mirage of a love fulfillment which lies always out of reach like a true Fata Morgana.

All sense of responsibility has fled from that man: responsibility toward the spirit within calling him to make of his outward actions the expression of an inward life, responsibility toward his fellow beings who become the tool and the pawn of his selfish desires, and responsibility toward the State which demands from its citizens new generations dedicated not to the pursuit of the ego's desires but to the service of the fatherland's needs.

We assist also to the laughable spectacle of the man who says: "There is no God," and who, having thought of God as of the policeman of his virtues, believes that his verbal rejection of a dreaded Power may open to him the door which leads to the path of unchecked pleasures.

We assist, yet, to the everyday spectacle of the business man damning the interference of the State in his affairs, and dreaming of a time when he can be completely free to pursue his goal of ruthless monetary gains.

We assist, finally, to the spectacle of great industrial, banking, and other powerful vested interests which, controlling the State as they do today, are enabled to exploit in a most inhuman and selfish way the common man's life.

The signs of the times are very eloquent indeed. They cry out aloud that the current view of human life, of its meaning, its purpose and its goal, cannot but lead to chaos and despair and to the ultimate downfall of western civilization.

When the gulf dividing those who have from those who have not has become so wide and deep as to be unabridgeable any longer; when those whose existence is only the shadow of a true human life are on the point of rebelling against the few who make of this existence such a hell on earth; when the rampant communist propaganda has taught the masses that there is only one way to end the martyrdom of the common man at the hands of his few more powerful because more fortunate brethren, and that this way is the way of destruction, of hate, and of death; when the only ideal worth fighting for has become the ideal of a society of ants or bees, dividing equally all wealth, all effort and all reward; when the opinion now being advanced that there is no God worth worshiping, no Family worth living for, no Fatherland worth dying for, has become a generalized and thoroughly accepted belief; a great step will have been accomplished then on the road which leads man backward from his present state to the primitive state of an animal among animals, concerned with his bodily needs, oblivious of the call of the Spirit, deaf to the voice of conscience.

The picture may seem entirely too black to be of possible realization. But stranger things than the fulfillment of this dire prophecy have taken place in the history of Man!

We must never forget that other civilizations of far greater significance than ours from the standpoint of spiritual achievements—the only true standard of comparison possible—have appeared on this earth, flowered forth in magnificent products of spiritual expression and disappeared again, engulfed in the shadows of oblivion and covered by few layers of sand or by the triumphant vegetation of the earth.

A new dark age is still possible, and it will dawn upon us soon enough unless we find again a meaning for life, a different purpose than the satisfaction of the senses, and, finally, a new goal for our efforts, nowadays so implacably frustrated by the emptiness, the vacuity, and the futility of the goal which we try so desperately and still so vainly to reach.

It is the possibility of such a Dark Age which Fascism is trying strenuously and successfully to stave off by teaching us anew the truth that we need to visualize and to worship a deeper reality lying behind and beyond the immediate and closely bound world of the self, if we want to find peace, achieve salvation and restore dignity and purpose to our life.

At this extremely critical time of our history, when the fate of a whole civilization is at stake, Fascism takes up once again the challenge and to the perplexing, ages-old query, it answers emphatically that life HAS a meaning, that it has a purpose and a goal, and that it has worth and dignity and beauty.

When we shall become aware that our individuality is truly and fully realized in those institutions and through those institutions called the Family, the Church, the Nation, and the State, then and only then, we shall realize the great significance and the deep import of the Fascist philosophy of life.

Fascism maintains in effect that the meaning of life is found only in the realization of a full life of the Spirit; that this realization in turn is achieved only when the individual's spiritual needs, aspirations and longings are rooted, integrated and nurtured in the Family, the Church, the Nation and the State; that these institutions, forming the framework of all life of the Spirit, enjoy in turn an existence of their own: timeless and absolute, whose essence partakes of the Spirit itself and is not contingent upon the Will and the actions of man.

In the Fascist philosophy of life Man first rises to the capacity of a true spiritual being when in the Family he finds something in which and through which he can express and realize his first spiritual needs—then in the church, an institution which offers him a new outlet for those spiritual needs not satisfied by the Family. Next, in the Nation, he finds something which expresses the fundamental continuity of his human experience within determinate limits of space, and the fundamental unity which is at the very root of life. Finally, in the State he finds an organism which gives ample scope to the expression of his spiritual life, an organism born of the conscious act of restricting, of his own free will, the full play of his activity and the full extent of his freedom; to allow his own rights, his own liberties, his own opportunities, to those fellow beings bound by the same laws, the same duties, the same authority.

The Family, the Church, the Nation, the State, these are the four cardinal points of the life of man; through them this life can flower forth in an expression of great spiritual achievement; denying them it can only revert to a state of satisfied animal wants unworthy of the name of human.

Hundreds of quotations from the works of Fascist thinkers could be selected, to be added here to substantiate this highly characteristic Fascist interpretation of the relationship of the individual to these four cardinal institutions. It will suffice, I believe, to report a few from the works of Balbino Giuliano and Giovanni Gentile.

"The Family—Giuliano maintains—as the basic element of society, has a purpose which goes beyond the reproduction of life and has to do with the first formation of the physical and spiritual structure of the individual.

"The Nation is the fundamental form of differentiation of the Spirit, the permanent continuity underlying the changes of the Spirit's creative activity; the concrete expression which must delimit and determine human universality if this abstraction is to achieve actual life. Outside of the concrete life of a nation there is neither humanity nor the human individual, because the individual is only and truly human when it is part of a nation from which it receives both thought and languages, memories and ideals: all the spiritual wealth, in short, which constitutes the most intimate part of his personality.

"The State is an organized collectivity which originates within the heart of the individual . . . when he realizes that an intimate affinity of spirit and a fundamental identity of interests bind him to other individuals . . . when he realizes that this organized collectivity constitutes the super-human entity in which lies the the innermost essence of his personality and his ideals . . . when he feels the need of imposing upon himself laws which restrict his activity in the interest of the common weal . . . when he creates a power which stands to represent the supreme authority of the institution and to enforce the obedience and the respect of Law."

And Giovanni Gentile says, "The individual, who in the innermost depth of his will is the very will of the State in the synthesis of the two terms: authority and liberty, is also the individual who through this will finds the solution of his moral and religious problems. . . . And for the catholic man this solution is found only living within the Church and under its discipline. Hence the need of the Fascist State to recognize the religious authority of the Church, to achieve the realization of the very aims of the State."

In conclusion, if man, to achieve salvation, must be led anew to visualize and worship a deeper reality than the immediate and closely bound world of the self, there is one way, and one way only to lead him to the goal, says Fascism, and that way is through the renewed cult of the Family, the Church, the Nation and the State.

This cult will give anew a meaning to life; with

this cult life will again find a purpose; through this cult life will finally reach its far off, magnificent goal which is nothing less than the spiritualization of man.

CHAPTER IV

FASCISM AND THE CONDUCT OF LIFE

Any theory or any practical system of life can be, in the end, justified only by life itself.

Only inasmuch as that theory or that system makes life better, richer, fuller, can there be any claim to an enduring fame conceded.

It is thus when we contrast the life of the country where Fascism has had its birth in the years immediately preceding this birth and the years following it, that we become especially considerate of the claims of Fascism to world recognition.

It is now beyond dispute and commonly conceded even by its fiercest adversaries that Fascism has transformed the life of Italy. A new spirit is permeating all the strata of society, the breath of a new renaissance is stirring the old country to its deepest chords. The expectation of something great, of something wonderful yet to come, and ready to come, is there in the air galvanizing all the energies of the nation in one supreme expression of power. And the suspense can only increase the tension and add to the dynamical effects of that release of pent up energies, when such a release will occur.

Such being the facts, it remains of paramount importance for us to discover the secret cause of the success of Fascism, and learn whether that secret cause can be at work in a larger field of action, and bring about thus a deeper and wider influence in the life of mankind.

The conduct of life cannot be left to the individual choice of the people; cannot be dependent from their individual likes and dislikes; it must be, instead, determined for them by a power which is above them and comprehends them: namely, the State. Because upon the State rests the duty and the task of the fulfillment of the national ideal, because the State alone is conscious of the ends and the aims of the nation's life.

This cardinal tenet of Fascism fully realized in practice as well as in theory, brings to a close the whole period of human history characterized by the belief in Man and his powers; that period begun with the Reformation, leading to the French Revolution and the Declaration of the rights of Man, and ending, finally, with the present state of chaos and despair of the modern world.

The conduct of life must rest upon three great, unalterable principles—Fascism maintains—namely: the principle of Unity, the principle of Authority and the principle of Duty.

"One invisible tie binds together the destinies of all the people of one nation. There cannot be any joy or any pain experienced by one single individual, any good or any evil befallen to him which shall not ultimately affect the welfare of the whole nation."

This is the first principle of the Fascist conduct of life, and one whose consequences prove to be the most far-reaching in the life of a nation.

If we have found always, says Fascism, such shifting grounds for the foundations of a durable and satisfactory social life, it is simply because we have forgotten that the good of the whole cannot be dependent from the material welfare of the individual, that the very life of the individual is dependent upon and is part of the life of an entity much greater and of far deeper meaning than his small ego, namely, the nation of which he is an integral part and which constitutes for him the supreme essence of the race.

Never before, to be sure, had a social and political system advanced such claims upon the inner world of man as this claim of Fascism to determine for him the forms of conduct; never before has that regeneration of social and political life, always dreamed, never effectuated, been so close to realization.

The first principle of the Fascist conduct of life rests upon a mystic belief of the oneness of all living beings; the second principle, the principle of Authority, rests upon another mystic belief: that of the divine essence of the hero. Not the military hero, but hero in the sense meant by Carlyle: hero of the soul.

"Find in any country the ablest man that exists there, raise him to the supreme place and loyalty, reverence him, you have a perfect government for that country; no ballot box, parliamentary eloquence, voting, constitution building or other machinery whatsoever can improve it a whit. It is the perfect State, the ideal Country."

Thus spoke Carlyle in his lecture on the hero as king, delivered the twenty-second of May, 1840. And his words are no less true today than they were a hundred years ago. Nay, still closer to the truth, if that could be possible, and true in a still deeper sense than Carlyle ever thought. Because the ultimate reality of the Universe which lies behind and beyond the deceiving realm of appearances, does not reveal itself indiscriminately and equally to all men.

There is Man in the abstract as a thinking and spiritual being; there are men in the concrete gifted in various degrees with the gifts of these divine elements of thought and soul.

We are all partakers of the divine, but the Hero among us is partaker of it in a fuller measure than all. He is in a more direct, more immediate relationship with the fountain-head of all knowledge, all wisdom, all love. What He sees in life we do not see, and it is even useless for us to strive toward a better comprehenion of life, a better understanding of nature, because we shall never be able to render asunder the veil of mystery shrouding the ultimate aspect of reality.

Vainly we strive through observation, experimentation, analysis, logic, to reach the core of being. The highest truths are hidden from us. Only that magic flash of a moment of supreme intuition,

70

that flash which renders for an instant man akin to God, can reveal the Truth. And we shall never know the ecstasy of that moment. The supreme gifts of synthesis, intuition, revelation, are denied to us; they belong rightly to the hero and to none other.

And if there is no hero in a country, darkness is upon the land; the darkness originating from the confusion of conflicting ideas, conflicting beliefs, conflicting wills.

It can be realized then at once how utterly impossible it is to conciliate such an article of faith with a naive belief in the wisdom of the mass, the leadership of the many, the supreme worth of Democracy,

The day may come, perhaps, and we all sincerely hope and pray for it, when all men will be heroes, but at the present stage of human evolution, let only the greatest among the great rule and govern, because he sees deeper and further than we shall ever be able to see. because he knows what we shall never be able to know, because He is a gift from God.

But if the principle of Authority recognizes that ultimately there must be a supreme power, it is, nevertheless, not completely exhausted by this recognition. Fascism holds, in fact, that the State must be a social, political, economic, moral and religious organism built as a pyramid at whose vertex is the national hero, the greatest man of his time and his nation, and leading to this national hero by an uninterrupted series of continuously widening powers arranged in hierarchies.

The hierarchy becomes thus the very essence of

Authority and the hierarchical arrangement of Society its truest expression in the world of man.

All the recognition of a man's worth is expressed in the place he occupies in the hierarchy; all the functions of a man's social and political life are contained in the functions he must fulfill as a member of the hierarchy.

No man is an outcast in the social system of Fascism, no man is worthless; no man, that is, who belongs to the Fascist nation and to its life.

It is, therefore, not the smallest title of glory of Fascism to have brought about this new realization of the fellowship of man at a time held, by common consent, to be a time of supreme and inevitable moral decadence.

But these two great principles of the unity of all human beings and of devotion to authority as expressed through a scale of human values, cannot be separated—Fascism holds—from the third and greatest principle of all: the principle of Duty.

And it is, perhaps, in this conception of duty as supreme motive power of the actions of man, and in the belief that such a conception can be transformed into living reality, that Fascism reveals most clearly the profound idealism underlying its philosophy.

There are some fundamental laws to which Man's moral nature must inevitably conform itself, and according to which the conduct of Man's life upon this earth must take place, if this life is to fulfill its high purpose, says Fascism.

It is commonly thought that these laws are derived from the pragmatic results of human behavior. No thought is, perhaps, farther from the truth than this. Those laws were originally, and still are, at the basis of the very constitution of the Universe, and Man's moral nature will be progressively fashioned in the process of ages in such a way as to render Man able to conform himself to them. To supersede those laws will prove always in the end to be an utterly vain attempt, because any human effort or process that runs contrary to the eternal order of things, as existing in the realm of the Absolute, must needs come to naught.

And because every moral law pre-exists in the realm of the Absolute, as a timeless manifestation of the Spirit, it is only necessary for Man to discover in himself possibilities of further moral progress that the Divine Idea may become embodied in a Human Law, and the Ideal become Reality.

It was therefore, inevitable, holds Fascism, that sooner or later Man in his moral progress should have discovered and applied to its practical life the principle of Duty.

Man is gifted with Reason and is gifted with a social capacity. He has made so far full use of his first gift. It is high time, Fascism says, that he realizes all the possibilities contained within the second.

Man, in other words, must be awakened to that sense of responsibility toward his fellow being which is comprehended under the name of Duty. And until this sense of responsibility is entirely awakened and active in his life, he is not entitled to the name of Man.

In common with all the animal kingdom, Man possesses his rights, but, alone in the Universe He is bound to recognize Duty.

This doctrine of Duty is clearly the heritage of the thought of Mazzini.

Next to Dante in importance, although not next to him in the process of time, is, for Fascism and its philosophy, the great apostle of the Italian "Risorgimento," Giuseppe Mazzini.

If Dante has left his legacy to Fascism the conception of the historical mission of Rome, the vision of a world empire as the only means of bringing about perpetual peace, the consciousness of the intimate relationship between the world of God and the world of Man; Mazzini, on the other hand, has left as his legacy this most radical of all thoughts, viz; that social life can find its true expression only when, to the theory of Right, the individual substitutes and adopts the theory of Duty.

No more far reaching and revolutionary words than these were ever heard by the modern world:

"Right is the faith of the individual. Duty is the common collective faith. Right can but organize resistance; it may destroy, it cannot found. Duty builds up, associates and unites; it is derived from a general law, whereas, Right is derived only from human will. There is nothing therefore to forbid a struggle against Right; any individual may rebel against any right in another which is injurious to him; and the sole judge left between the adversaries is Force.

"Societies based upon Duty would not be compelled to have recourse to Force; Duty, once admitted as the rule excludes the possibility of struggle; and by rendering the individual subject to the general aim, it cuts at the very root of those evils which Right is unable to prevent, and only affects to cure.

"The doctrine of Rights puts an end to sacrifice and cancels martyrdom from the world; in every theory of individual rights, interests become the governing and motive power and martyrdom an absurdity, for what interests can endure beyond the tomb!"

Life thus, as conceived by Fascism, is "serious, austere, religious, and its development takes place in a world sustained by the moral and responsible forces of the spirit."

This means, in turn, that to be a Fascist it is, of all things, the most difficult in the world. He who subscribes to the doctrine of Fascism subscribes also to rules of conduct which make exacting claims upon his will to live a satisfactory sensual life. The life of the Fascist is a life of ascetic self-denial, heroic self-sacrifice, moral abnegation and religious enthusiasm.

The true Fascist works not for himself alone, but for his nation as well; believes not in a godless Universe, but in a universe which exists by the will of God; worships this God not as a remote, abstract entity having no intimate connection with his individual life, but as something from which he parted at birth, to which he can confidently appeal in life and which he shall rejoin at death; the true Fascist forsakes the realization of his rights for the fulfillment of his duties; strives to make of love an expression of the soul rather than an enjoyment of the senses; holds the unity of the family to be a sacred thing and monogamic marriage to be the supreme test and the true end of love; respects that hierarchical arrangement of society which, through successive stages, confers the primary Authority of divine origin to men invested with power to rule over their fellow beings; is willing to sacrifice his personal pleasure for the welfare of his brethren, willing to suffer for the welfare of his family, willing to die for the welfare of his country and, finally, the true Fascist is willing to forego all claims to personal freedom if these claims conflict with the realization of the true goal of life: the spiritualization of man.

Will the Fascist efforts devoted to such a great aim as a spiritual leavening of human life be crowned by success? The day when man believes and acts as a truly moral being, recognizing no other law of life greater than the moral law, may still dawn then.

"Few are those writers who have been bold enough to affirm that Fiscism is essentially a mystic-religious movement
—N. Coco.

CHAPTER V

FASCIST ETHICS

"Fascism rejects the doctrine of Materialism and any other doctrine which attempts to explain the intricate history of human societies from the narrow and exclusive standpoint of the preeminence of material interests."

These words of Mussolini on the sixth of January, 1923, must need be considered as the prolegomena of all Fascist philosophy. They characterize at once this new system of philosophy making its appearance in the realm of thought, as essentially a new form of Idealism.

Fascist philosophy, as evolved by its most representative thinkers, begins, in fact, with the explicit recognition of the fundamental, irreducible duality of Reality, the duality Subject-Object.

This recognition, when it is not vivified by a still higher philosophic principle, leads to an impasse wthout solution, or with solutions characterized by contradictions and negations.

77

But the philosophy of Fascist thinkers having posited the existence of the duality Subject-Object, immediately resolves this duality through the recognition that all Reality, be it apparently external to us, or an integral part of ourselves, cannot be apprehended unless it is transformed into pure thought.

The synthesis: external world-data of experience —states of consciousness-mental process-thought, presupposes in turn the existence of the Idea.

The Idea is at bottom Reality itself, that is, Reality before its unity transformed itself into the duality Subject-Object, and after this duality resolves again into pure thought.

Thought becomes thus for Fascism the very criterion of Truth. "No aspect of Reality," writes a Fascist thinker, "can partake of the Truth which is outside of Thought."

Upon the foundations laid by this idealistic conception of Reality, Fascism builds the structure of its philosophy and, particularly, of its ethics which eagerly extend all their roots into the fertile soil of this new Idealism.

All Fascist theory of Ethics begins with the recognition that morality is always in the making, is never final. It is always in the making, because that process which resolves the apprehension of moral relationships of the external world into pure thought, goes on forever. Any and all of these relationships pre-exist as Ideas in the realm of the Absolute; in that realm, that is, which lies outside of time and space, but become thought in a realm which is essentially characterized by the sequence of time.

Furthermore, morality is never final because the human mind cannot but rise through slow, successive and never-ending stages to that plane where pure thought partakes of the character of the Absolute.

Morality, therefore, must accept the external world as it presents itself to the apprehension of the intellect, it cannot fashion for itself an arbitrary external world of moral values and moral relationships projected out of the mind. And the field of Ethics is not the legislation of arbitrary laws of morality, but the transformation into laws, through the process of thought, of the moral relationships which man discovers existing in the external world at a given time and place. Viewed in this light all moral issues, all moral problems acquire a new significance.

The paramount moral problem is, obviously, the problem of good and evil. All efforts to deny the existence of evil in the world of man and the world of nature, have resolved themselves into a misinterpretation of the very essence of life itself.

"What is life, in effect?" asks Fascism, and its answer is that life is at bottom only and simply a state of equilibrium always reached, always broken; the moment in which that equilibrium becomes final, that moment marks the passing of life and the appearance of death.

Good and evil are thus the primary conditions of the very existence, the very possibility of life. Fascist Ethics, which, like all systems of Ethics, is above all concerned with good and evil; does not deny them, but accepts them while they present themselves as subjects of thought, and builds upon them its structure of individual and social morality.

In the words of Mussolini:

"Strife is the origin of all things, for life is full of contrasts; there is love and hate, white and black, night and day, good and evil, and until these contrasts are reduced to an equilibrium, strife will always remain at the root of human nature, like a supreme fatality. . . . And on the whole it is well that it is so."

Of social morality the problem of war and peace is undoubtedly the paramount problem. Much has been written since immemorial time of the evil of war and the good of peace so much that to approach the subject anew means simply to fall into banal repetition.

And, yet, it is especially in the consideration of this problem that the originality of Fascist philosophy is clearly shown.

In the light of Fascist philosophy the eternal problem of war and peace acquires a deeper meaning and receives a strikingly characteristic solution.

If it is true, in fact, that all life is, at bottom, nothing more than a state of equilibrium forever destroyed, forever renewed, then it is also true that the very possibility of its realization on the earth implies the perpetuation in time and space of this duality of warring elements of construction and destruction. The moment that the duality resolves into unity with the temporary triumph of one of the two fundamental elements, that moment marks also the passing of life and the appearance of death.

And what is true for the individual is so much more true for the life of a nation. Nations may be said to live fully, indeed, only in those rare moments of history when the constructive forces have reached their zenith, and the destructive forces have not as yet begun to disintegrate the social structure.

Those rare moments justify all the years of patient preparation, of laborious building, of unsung sacrifices. Yes, everything is justified which helps to bring about the realization of such moments: even war, if war is necessary. Because, what prices life is not peace, but life itself. And death must not be mistaken for peace.

In the words of the father of Fascism:

"... the doctrine of pacifism is born of a renunciation of the struggle and an act of cowardice in the face of sacrifice."

Such is the warring creed of Fascism resounding strangely solitary in a world grown weary of the horrors of war, as though war were not an integral part of the drama of its existence and without that drama this existence had any meaning at all.

"Humanity is yet, and will always be, an abstraction in time and space," said Mussolini on January 2, 1921, "Men are not brothers, neither do they want to be, and evidently they cannot be.

"Peace is hence absurd, or, rather, is a necessary pause in the process of war. There is something that binds man to his destiny of struggling either against his fellows or against himself. The motives for the struggle may change indefinitely, they may be economical,

81

religious, political, sentimental, but the legacy of Cain and Abel seems to be the inescapable reality, while brotherhood is a fable to which men listen between the bivouac and the truce."
And on the sixth of February, 1922, he said:

"I must acknowledge that I do not believe in eternal peace. . . . In this world there are some fundamental facts called race, progress, development, rise and decline of peoples; facts all leading to conflicts which often cannot be resolved in any other way than through armed force."

One year later he is still more emphatic.

"I see the world as it actually is; that is a world of unbridled egoism. Were the world a pastoral Arcadia, it would be a very pleasant and beautiful thing to spend the time among the nymphs and the shepherds. But I do not see this Arcadia. And even when I look at the great flags of great principles fluttering in the wind, I do not fail to perceive that behind those flags, more or less hallowed, are hidden egotistic interests seeking their place in the sun."

Such a profoundly realistic vision of the actual circumstances of life appears, at first thought, to lead to pessimism and despair. It remains, therefore, a great title of glory of Fascism that of having been able to pass from this vision to a higher synthesis, a synthesis of inspiring soul-building Idealism.

War is neither good nor evil—Fascism says— War is an experience of the race; an experience justified and explained by the whole historical process which has made of mankind the social, moral and political organism of our times. If peace is the primary condition of the possibility of such a process, so is war. Perpetual peace means the end of all competition, the want of all ambition, the defeat of all efforts; it means, in short, lethargy instead of activity, regress instead of progress, death instead of life.

We must have the courage—says Fascism—to affirm, in a world grown weary of the horrors of war, that it is given to man to rise above those horrors whenever war becomes necessary to the triumph of an Ideal. To die or to suffer for such a triumph is not to die or to suffer at all, it is to live forever.

This clear recognition of the peculiar relationship of national groups with their fundamental incompatible national antagonisms — antagonisms which are at the very basis and, perhaps, the very condition of the greater life of mankind—resolves thus into a call to heroism, a call to a renewal of the heroic spirit in man which alone can give dignity to his illusory, transitory, aimless, and so poignantly unsatisfactory life.

The very problem of suffering, of the apparently great and needless amount of grief and pain in the universe, is shadowed by the recognition of Fascism that only through sorrow are we able to apprehend the higher things of life. And he who suffers is not to be pitied, but envied.

The issue is very clear.

"It amounts to choose," said Mussolini on

February 5th, 1924, "between the false theories of life and history, and our square Roman Latin spirit, which can take account of the whole Reality, which faces life as a continuous struggle, and is ready and willing to die when the Idea calls and the great bell of history rings."

Next to the relationship between national groups, it is also the concern of Ethics the relationship between the individual and Society. And here again the principles of Fascist Ethics are definitely original in their recognition of the fundamental character of such a relationship.

Fascist Ethics begins, in fact, with the acknowledgement that it is not the individual who confers a meaning upon society, but it is, instead, the existence of a human society which determines the human character of the individual.

In the Fascist philosophy, in other words, man is shifted from his privileged position at the center of the whole universe, and his place is occupied by mankind, or, rather, by that collective expression of mankind called Nation.

"Individuality cannot become the basis of sociality without setting itself at war with all that is included in the meaning of individuality."

These words of a Fascist thinker explain the whole attitude of Fascist Ethics toward the individual's claims and its maximum concern for the fullest expression of the nation's life.

It is necessary to subordinate the individual to

the family—says the same thinker: Antonio Pagano, in his book "Idealismo e Nazionalismo"—the family to civil society and, finally, Society to the State. Only in this way, through such a process, the material being is transformed into an ethical individual, into a person; and, from being simply part of a physical universe, becomes a cell of the moral universe."

And herein lies all the profound significance of Fascist Ethics: in a re-valuation, that is, of that primary fundamental relationship of life which is the relationship Man-God-Universe.

Finally, when faced by the issue of the relationship of Man to his fellow beings, Fascism rises to the vision of that future state of Society; that state in which man shall not attempt to enslave his brethren, shall not erect himself as their master, but shall, instead, do whatever is in his power to elevate them to that higher level of consciousness where Ethical norms reign supreme.

"The slaves are no longer below us, they are among us."

This sad reflection of Amiel epitomizes the condition of the modern world throughout that whole period of history opened by the Industrial Revolution, and only now coming to a close in the Italian peninsula:—a period characterized by man's brutish subservience to the machine, by the progressive impoverishment of all his spiritual traits, by the rise of the great god "Business," by the forsaking of Tradition, by the negation of the Past, by the degeneration of Love.

That we have amongst us countless slaves who

are chained to a life-time of meaningless drudgery, to the monotonous, mechanical repetition of a performance of daily tasks from which all soul has fled, we cannot deny.

But what we hardly realize is that the number of slaves has been constantly growing and threatens to engulf us all, threatens to drown whatever few free human spirts still remain.

Clearly, unless we restore to all these millions of human beings—robbed of their very soul—their right to create life as they go on living, they will bring mankind to the doom of a mechanical existence devoid of all values, all meaning.

We must, in other words, restore the urge to creative activity to the artist and the artisan alike; we must restore the power to shape his own destiny to every individual; we must restore the possibility to give always newer forms to personal and social life; we must make again of man what he was meant to be: a being gifted with the divine gift of creative power, using this power to make of his life a creation of beauty.

And what we all must do sooner or later, throughout the world, Fascism is already doing now in Italy.

Fascism, in re-establishing the claim of the artisan to make of his work an expression of his soul, is attempting to restore to the individual the lost consciousness of his creative power, and to Society the material out of which all Art, all Literature and all Religion is born.

The norms of Fascist Ethics are thus not norms abstract from life, but part and parcel of the very substance of life, and, as such, true reflections in the transitory world of man, of one of the aspects of the timeless world of Ideas.

CHAPTER VI

FASCISM AND LIBERTY

The Fascist conception of life is so radically revolutionary in all its aspects as to justify an extended individual treatment of each one of these aspects in a detailed analysis.

As we have already seen, the general, all-embracing conception is that life is an expression of the soul, and, as such, flowering at its best only when its spiritual claims are fully recognized and satisfied.

Now the nature of these claims is such that they conflict inevitably with all the individual's egotistic aspirations, ambitions and desires.

The Fascist conception of life advances, therefore, demands upon the inner world of man, that the ordinary human being is wary to satisfy. It is from this contrast between the claims of the individual and the claims of the whole that the problem of Liberty arises. Because Fascism finds necessary, at the outset, to take away from the ordinary human being what he has been taught and

89

has grown to cherish the most: personal liberty. And it can be affirmed, without falling into exaggeration, that a curtailment of personal liberty not only has proved to be, but must necessarily be, a fundamental condition of the triumph of Fascism.

Unfortunately, it is just due to such a curtailment that the greatest misunderstanding of Fascism has arisen in the world where personal liberty is made almost the paramount issue of life.

But Fascism holds that personal liberty is not an end to itself. Personal liberty is simply a means to the realization of a much greater end: namely, the liberty of the Spirit; this last meaning the faculty of the human Soul of rising above the power of outward circumstances and inward needs to devote itself to the cult of those ideals which form the true goal of life.

Two radically different conceptions of Liberty are thus in conflict, and there is no hope that the abyss which separates them can ever be bridged.

In the Fascist conception, to be free, means to be no more a slave to one's own passions, ambitions or desires; means to be free to will what is true, and good and just, at all times, in all cases; means, in other words, to realize here in this world the true mission of man.

In the Individualistic conception, instead, to be free is . . . to follow the call of one's own nature; to worship one's own God; to think, to act, or to speak according to the dictates of one's own mind; to earn, to spend, to save or to hoard at will; to accumulate property and deed it following one's own whims or fancy; to reach all edonistic goals; wealth, health, happiness or pleasure. In other words, to be unhindered by compulsions, restrictions, prohibitions, rules, codes and laws.

In this conception Liberty takes, as Spengler says:

> ". . . the bloody significance that has in the declining ages. What is meant is: Liberation from all bonds of Civilization, from every kind of form and custom; pride and quietly borne poverty, silent fulfillment of duty, renunciation for the sake of a task or conviction, greatness in enduring one's fate, loyalty, honour, responsibility, achievements, all this a constant reproach to the humiliated and insulted."

What the Individualistic conception of Liberty implies is thus nothing less than freedom from all those external fetters born of the very fact that man is forced to live in a state of society; a state, that is, which makes fundamental claims over all forms of individual freedoms, a state which places iron-clad restrictions to that form of Liberty which would would allow complete expression of his instincts, his desires and his needs.

But, as Giovanni Gentile says:

> "The only form of Liberty which knows no limits, no bounds, no restrictions, is the Liberty of the artist, inasmuch as Art is a dream which represents an abstraction from reality; that reality of which other men are part, and that comprises the world to which our life is bound. Art can thus spatiate in that free world of fancy where the individual is creator and lord of his own creations. And the artist is the be-

ing who seeks and finally finds that his Liberty is outside this world of ours, where there is Work and there is Sorrow, where there is the hard law, which limits the individual and where there is that force weighing down on man—a force superior to every natural or human force —which we may call God or Fate, and which no power of will or of science can ever win or efface."

Furthermore, the true facts are that although the fundamental instincts of man have remained —in his civilized state—practically the same ones to which he was slave in his natural state, his desires and his needs are not the same any longer but have increased a thousandfold, because they are born of the very increase of civilizing agents. And the more developed, the more complete, the more complex a civilization becomes, the more it offers in the way of comfort, attraction, pleasure, the more does the individual become a slave of increased needs, or increased desires. Those wants which man found in the state of nature already difficult to satisfy fade now in importance when compared to the infinitely more numerous wants originating from his reaction to that artificial environment we call civilization. If, in the state of nature, he was only yearning to be free to eat at satiety whenever it pleased him, to roam at will, and to love whenever his animal nature required it; now, in his civilized state, Man is yearning to be free to worship, to think, to win and keep a home, to rear children, to earn, to spend, to save, to accumulate property. . . .

Whatever freedom, in other words, he was yearning for in his state of nature, ought to be increased a thousandfold to match the freedom he is yearning for in his present state.

But, as in his natural state, Man was not free to eat at satiety whenever it pleased him, to roam at will or to love whenever he felt the call of his animal nature, because he found in his way obstacles which he could not overcome, so it happens also that this instinctive yearning for unbounded freedom to reach, to obtain and to keep all the good things which civilization parades before his eyes, cannot be satisfied and he must content himself at all times with only a partial realization of his wishes.

And, even, admitting that scientific progress and national economic planning were to make it possible for each and every individual to come in possession of a reasonable amount of material comfort, it still remains true that it is in the very nature of man that he is not at any time satisfied with his present condition and, therefore, his yearning to earn more, spend more, save more, accumulate more property, will still and always gnaw at his heart and make him wish for that magic freedom which is not of this world, or, at least, not of the world in its civilized state.

Truly freedom, absolute unrestricted freedom, is not the child of Liberty, but the mother of Anarchy; and as such is not the viatic of a true cultured state, but its mortal enemy.

A true cultured state means a state of society in which ethical values reign supreme, and ethical values presuppose, in all cases, limitations of individual freedom.

"As the fall of a stone in a quiet pool draws at the surface concentric circles which grow always wider in diameter until they extend to the extreme limits of the pool, thus the consequences of a human deed which seemed at first to affect the life of one man grow little by little to affect the life of all men."

In the light of this truth there is, or, rather, there ought to be, no being no earth who can do what he likes without taking heed of the consequences wrought by his thoughts, his words, or his actions; and if there is such a being he is not worthy of the name of Man.

Every human being, in fact, finds himself facing at every instant of his life, the dilemma whether the satisfaction of a certain desire, a certain instinct, or a certain need, conflicts with the welfare of his fellow beings, and whether or not he ought to bring about the realization of such a satisfaction irrespective of its ultimate consequences.

It is in the making of this decision; it is in the act of choosing not what he knows he desires, likes, or needs, but what his conscience tells him he ought to choose, even if this choice means suffering, disgrace, martyrdom, or death, that a human being becomes worthy of the name of Man. Then, and only then, he rises to the vision of the true role, the understanding of the true meaning, and the knowledge of the true function of Liberty.

Then, and only then, the words of Amiel can appear to him full of significance and he can give the affirmative answer to the pregnant question of the Swiss thinker:

"Is not responsibility the ultimate root of the being of Man?"

In this world of inter-related human activities, there is no place left for the explication of the free expression of individual personality; there is only place for the expression of this same personality as seen in the light of its relationship to the activities of other beings and true Liberty is that Liberty of the Spirit which alone can free us of all bounds, all fetters, all chains born from the world of nature and substitute to them those originating from the vision and the realization of the moral Law in the world of Man.

Only inasmuch as a political and social system denies to Man his inalienable right to this form of liberty is that political and social system guilty before God and before Man.

Fascism denies not such a right but affirms it, and not only affirms it but makes of it its supreme concern. Were the individual conscious of Man's great mission in the world; were the ordinary human being conscious of the aim and the meaning of human life; were he, in other words, master of his own self, there should be no need of agencies external to its own conscience to prescribe for him his course of action. Knowing exactly how to use his freedom for the furthering of the best aim of mankind; for the furthering of the good life, that is, the life of the spirit, the individual would then be left without other restrictions and demands on his freedom than those springing from his inner world.

But it is a fact, a conclusively proved historical fact, that the ordinary human being DOES NOT KNOW how to use his freedom, or rather he knows simply how to use it for the satisfaction of his instincts and desires.

And it is only because he finds himself compelled to live in a state of society that restrains him from bringing to its logical conclusion his assumption that the individual is the center of the whole universe.

All through the ages his life has been thus a sorry compromise between his desire to self expression and the need of curbing this desire if some kind of social life had to be realized at all.

It is high time, instead, says Fascism, that the individual be brought back to the vision of his true place in the universe; it is high time that he learns how to curb and master his self; it is high time that his freedom be taken away from him if he is to realize the greatest aim of life: the furtherance of the Spirit.

The day that he has learned how to master his own destiny, that day will sign for man his title to freedom, complete, unbound freedom, and will mark thus for him the birth to his true manhood.

Man must become, therefore, the master of his own self, master of his own fate. This is the call and the challenge of our times; this is the message of Fascism. To rise above the power of outward circumstances and inward needs; to heed the call of the Spirit; to bring forth the divine in him, must be the true goal of Man's efforts.

To pit himself alone against the cruel world of his animal nature; against the evil power of his fellow beings; against fate even, if necessary; against everything that tends to bend him, to crush him, to stifle him in his aspiration toward the good life; yes, this is the duty and the glory of Man.

Because if man can only be what he is at present, if there is no hope of realizing the good life, then what Nietzsche said becomes supremely true and:

"Man is something that must be surpassed."

Man must realize then with Fascism that this freedom is not an end in itself, but a means to an end; or, in the words of Mussolini:

"Liberty is not a right but a duty."

Such being the principles inspiring Fascism, all attempts of Fascist thinkers to clarify and justify the attitude of Fascism in regard to the problem of liberty are superfluous and would not even be worth the pain to report them, were it not that it is possible to detect through them the constant preoccupation to give a theoretical reason for what was instinctively felt.

We must never forget that the realization of the Idea Fascism antedates all attempts to understand such a realization in the light of reason.

But we shall again follow the struggle of the Idea toward its expression in some of the most characteristic utterances of Fascist thinkers. The first in order of time and importance is the one already reported by Mussolini on November 27, 1922, when he says:

"Liberty is not a right but a duty."
The following year on October 24, he says:
"Liberty without order and without discipline means dissolution and catastrophe."
And on the twenty-eighth of the same month:
"If for Liberty it is meant to stop the rhythm calm and orderly of the work of the nation; if for Liberty it is meant the right to insult the symbols of Religion, Fatherland and State; then, I declare as Head of the government and Duce of Fascism, that such a Liberty will never be."

It is possible to detect in these words the preoccupation generated by the undisciplined state of Italy before the rise of Fascism and the attempts to renew such a state during the first month of the Fascist regime.

They cannot be, therefore, of universal appeal. But the following one, pronounced the twenty-fourth of March, 1924, is timeless and of catholic application:

"The concept of Liberty is not an absolute concept, because in human life there is nothing absolute. Liberty is not a right, but a duty—is not a concession but a conquest—is not a symptom of equality, but of privilege. The concept of equality changes with the changes of times. There is a liberty of the times of peace which is not a liberty of war-times. There is a liberty of times of wealth which cannot be allowed in times of misery and depression. Finally, there is the great silent, continuous struggle; the struggle between the State and the Individual; between the State which demands and the Individual who attempts to evade such demands. Because the individual, left to himself, unless he be a saint or a hero, always refuses to pay taxes, obey laws or go to war."

In this speech of Mussolini, the relationship existent between the degree of freedom allowed to the individual and the higher claims of the State, receives for the first time full recognition. But this recognition goes far beyond this initial utterance. In the words of Fascist thinkers, the very first condition of the realization of the good life becomes identified with the condition of the supremacy of the State over the individual.

According to Fascism, a true, a great spiritual life cannot take place unless the State has risen to a position of pre-eminence in the world of man. The curtailment of liberty thus becomes justified at once, with this need of raising the State to its rightful position.

As Giovanni Gentile says, in his book—"What is Fascism!"—

"Liberty is, to be sure, the supreme end and aim of every human life, but insofar as personal and social education realize it by evoking this common will in the individual, it presents itself as law, and hence as the State. The maximum of liberty coincides with the maximum strength of the State." And, further on: "A state which presupposes liberty denies it precisely because it presupposes it, for there is no liberty outside of the life of the spirit, which, unlike natural beings, does not presuppose itself, but creates, conquers and evokes itself. A man BECOMES free; he is not so by nature. And the State is liberal in fact and not merely verbally, if it promotes the development of liberty considered as an ideal to be attained and not as a natural right to be guaranteed.

"And when the individual believes that were he enjoying liberty in the full meaning of the word, a blessed utopia would be instaurated in the world, Fascism answers through the words of one of its spokesmen: 'Individuality cannot become the basis of Sociality without setting itself at war with all that is included in the meaning of Individuality.' "

Liberty, therefore, cannot be concerned with the individual's claims, but must find its maximum concern in the fullest expression of the nation's life, and of the State which of such a life is the concrete realization.

"It is necessary to subordinate the individual to the Family," says another Fascist thinker, Antonio Pagano, in his book "Idealism and Nationalism," "the family to civil society and, finally, society to the State. Only in this way, through such a process, the material being is transformed in an ethical individual, in a person, and from being simply part of a physical universe, becomes a cell of the moral universe."

It is not the individual, thus, which confers a meaning to society, but it is the existence of a human society, the existence of the State, which determines the human character of the individual.

Giovanni Gentile expresses very forcefully this fundamental truth when he says:

"The Philosophy of Fascism denies that form of liberty which attempts to be outside the law, as only through the law, that is, the State, is it possible to realize its existence in the process of time in the best part of the conscience and the will of the citizen."

We are brought back to conceive Liberty through the classic definition of Montesquieu:

"Liberty is nothing else but the right to do only what the laws allow."

At the same time we see all the importance of personal freedom fade in contrast with the transcendent import of the realization of the Ideal of the Nation-State. And it is not the least title of glory of Mussolini to have seized since the very first the true mission of Fascism as mainstay of the Liberty of the State.

"The work of fifty years of history and, above all, the war, have made finally a nation out of the Italians. The historic task that awaits us is to make this nation into a national State. This is a MORAL IDEA which finds embodiment in a system of responsible hierarchies, whose members from the highest to the lowest feel the pride and the privilege of doing this particular duty. . . . Our one aim must be the erection of this single unified being: the Nation-State, the sole bearer of the whole history, the whole future and the whole power of the Italian people."

Thus wrote Mussolini in his paper "Il Popolo d'Italia" the second of January, 1923, setting to himself and to Fascism a program which was to stir a whole country to new life, and shall, perhaps in time, stir the whole western world.

"For the end of man on earth," says another Fascist thinker, Francesco Ercole, "is not to live blessed and inert in a paradise of identity of all men which would make life unworthy of being lived; it is, rather, to dedicate himself as an individual to the triumph of those national values which history entrusts to him for the sake of the progress of human civilization." And Mussolini again:

"The anti-individualistic Fascist conception of life is servant of the State and it takes only heed of the individual inasmuch as he is one with the State, which represents the conscience and the universal will of man in his historical existence. . . . Fascism is thus for the only serious form of Liberty, the Liberty of the State and of the individual within the State."

The prophecy of Elie Fauré, as told in those words with which this chapter opens, has been fulfilled by Fascism and the individual is thus brought back to merge himself and disappear if not in the multitude and the universe, in that collective expression of mankind which is the Nation-State.

PART TWO
FASCISM AS POLITICAL AND
ECONOMIC ORGANIZATION

CHAPTER VII

FASCISM AND DEMOCRACY

All possibilities of the realization of Democracy rest ultimately upon the implicit belief in the capacity of the common man to know what is good and beautiful and true; that is, upon a naive, unbound faith in his wisdom.

And because it has been generally assumed that wisdom can be taught, it was only natural to hope that in adequate time the common man would undoubtedly become a living embodiment of all intellectual and moral virtues.

And finally, because men in general believe to be true what they only hope to be true, the gospel of Democracy as the new Utopia found immediate acceptance and widespread diffusion.

The whole history of modern times may be characterized by the struggle, the temporary victory and the final defeat, to instaure the Kingdom of Democracy in the human society when this society was not ready—and is not, and will, perhaps never be—to let the common man be arbiter of his own and his brother's life.

But this phase of human history is drawing to a close, if it has not already drawn to its close. More and more clearly and forcefully we are coming to realize that we were and are deceiving ourselves, that narrow limitations constitute the boundaries of the spiritual, intellectual and moral life of the common man, that he is by nature enowed with instincts but not with wisdom, and that no amount of learning, instruction, education, can ever increase his human stature beyond the limits set to his possibilities at the very time of his birth.

Because we cannot learn except what we learn from within; that which is in tune with our deeper selves and can be assimilated and become food of that intangible and yet all pervading element of our personality: the spirit within.

Vainly we offer knowledge, education, wisdom, to the common man. He cannot benefit of our offer. Mother nature dotes her human children very sparingly of the higher gifts of intelligence, understanding, spirituality. Once in a long time she gives birth to a Buddha, a Confucius, a Plato, a Jesus, filling the whole world with visions of a higher life opening its realm to the access of man.

Then, perhaps exhausted by her effort, she falls back to her everyday role of begetter of mediocrities, and those visions of a higher life remain only dreams of men who shall never be able to realize them.

Such being the facts, it is almost criminal to keep alive in mankind the hope of a true realization of the Democratic ideal. By so doing, in fact, we preclude the possibility of a development of human society along paths more in tune with the needs, the aspirations and the possibilities inherent in the mass of men; men as they really are in nature: not as we wish them to be.

Fascism recognizes therefore at the outset that Democracy cannot be realized and that whenever and wherever it has been tried, it has degenerated sooner or later into an oligarchy of tyrannical autocrats—be they military, as of old, or financial, as of modern times.

To a bastard form of social and political organization, which like all bastard things, cannot last because of its inherent falsehood, Fascism substitutes a genuine life-enhancing organization sprung from the recognition of the fundamental truth of life: the truth that the mass of men is created to be governed and not to govern; is created to be led and not to lead, and is created, finally, to be slaves and not masters: slaves of their animal instincts, their physiological needs, their emotions and their passions.

A day may dawn, perhaps, when all men will be so many Socrates, but until that day dawns let us get rid of this great falsehood which is the Democratic Ideal, let us get rid of our hypocrisy, let us be sincere, let us acknowledge that the average man is unfit to rule his life and our life, let us resign ourselves to the rule of the best among us, for our good and for the good of the whole.

As Mussolini said the 17th of November, 1922:

"We want to uplift the people materially

and spiritually, but not because we think that
number, mass, quantity may create some special types of civilization in the future. We leave
this ideology to those who profess themselves
to be priests of this mysterious religion."

and on July 23, 1933:

"Democracy . . . lives by and for words . . .
But in times of crisis the people do not ask to
be propagandized . . . they wish to be com-
manded."

These words of Mussolini are the key to the
two-fold aspects of Fascism: characterized by its
lack of faith in the masses and its great aim of
uplifting their material and spiritual conditions.

What shall the Fascist State do then for the
countless beings constituting the pulsating, living
masses of people, with their ambitions and their
desires, their loves and their hates, their dreams
and their hopes?

What shall the Fascist State do for them and
what can it expect from them in return?

It is in the positing of such a question and in
its answer where Fascism differs most radically from
any political and social system of modern times—
because the whole outlook of Fascism on the role
played by the different individuals of a nation, is
based on a philosophical conception of the utmost
singularity and importance.

Fascism resolutely rejects that so often and so
vociferously repeated slogan that all men are created
equal.

Fascism holds instead that all men are created

unequal in intellectual, spiritual, moral and physical attributes.

What is common to all men is their humanity.

But just because of the fact that the supreme meaning of this common root overshadows the meaning of whatever differences might exist in those accessories of human personality which are thought, creative ability, artistic expression and so forth; just because of the fact that all men—whether they are intelligent or not, creators or interpreters, thinkers or laborers, artists or artisans, are nevertheless only and simply human beings, after all, Fascism holds that all the members of a nation must consider themselves to be nothing more than servants of one cause, giving correspondingly to their inborn possibilities, the full measure of their devotion to the triumph of this cause.

What mankind has lost thus with the loss of political democracy it has gained with a revenge in this new conception of a spiritual democracy where the greatest and the lowest have, in the eyes of the State, the same ultimate worth.

> "Men are not created equal but must act as though they were created equal."

Much of Fascism will disappear in time but this article of faith will become undoubtedly part of the spiritual heritage of Mankind.

In the light shed by the weighty implications of this basic philosophical Fascist conception of social life, the imposing edifice of recrimination against the outward political forms of Fascism; Dictatorship, Militarism, Hierarchy, etc., and of regrets for the lost familiar playthings of Democracy; ballot-box, representative government, etc., loses its definite outline and becomes a shadowy entity.

The criticism heaped thus at Fascism when it has been confused with Dictatorship has no foundation, because the two terms are not synonimous, because Fascism is something more, something infinitely greater than Dictatorship, because the Fascist peculiar form of political organization is nothing else but a tool necessary at present for the building up of a nation's life and because this tool may be used or discarded in turn as the occasion arises and the needs demand it, without affecting in the least the essential truth of Fascism.

If Authoritary rule, in other words, is temporarily a necessary element of Fascism, if Liberalism must be discarded for a new form of social theory, if Democracy is incompatible with the true political and social characteristics of mankind; it is nevertheless also true that Fascism does not imply necessarily Dictatorship, that Liberalism may still evolve so as to accept as fundamental reality of Life, the duality between the possibilities inherent to Man as individual and those inherent to Man as a social being and abandon forever its utopian belief in Man as master of the whole Universe and that, finally, the new Democracy may be enabled to select heroes for leaders; true heroes, not demagogic puppets, and become thus another form of Fascism under a different name.

But in its road to Canossa, the new Democracy must forego all the paraphernalia of outworn political forms if it is to become identified with Fascism at all, because Fascism has an utter contempt of those political forms in general and of parliaments in particular.

This distrust of parliaments, which only now has become general throughout the entire world, was voiced by F. T. Marinetti in Italy as early as 1910. "The parliamentary system is almost everywhere a wasted form," he said. "It gave us a few good results; created an illusory participation of the majority in the government; I say illusory because it is a proved fact that people cannot and will never be represented by representatives that they do not know how to select. The people, therefore, always remain outside the government."

And Mussolini, giving the reasons for this distrust, on the eighth of June, 1923 said: "Parliamentarism has been fatally wounded by two typical phenomena of our times: syndicalism and journalism. Syndicalism, because it concentrates in determinate associations, all the people having special and particular interests of their own to defend; Journalism, because it is the daily parliament, the daily rostrum where men coming from universities, industries, sciences, life itself, discuss all the problems with a knowledge which is rarely found upon the seats of a Parliament."

More forceful yet is another of Mussolini's speeches: "All over the world there is a feeling that the parliamentary system, a system which lasted for a number of decades in the history of the nineteenth century, has exhausted its usefulness and that today it is insufficient to deal with the growing impetus of the needs and passions of modern civilization. There is a feeling everywhere that in this modern society it is necessary to re-establish the principles of order, of discipline, of hierarchy, in all their severity, without which human society is headed for chaos and ruin."

But nowhere else is the case against Parliament stated so effectively as in the "Report of the Royal Commission for Constitutional reforms." "The parliamentary system is the gravest and most dangerous degeneration of political custom. It constitutes a complex deviation and usurpation of powers. It is not in harmony with the origins and historic bases of parliaments. It is evidently opposed to the logical demands of the constitutional and representative regime. And, what is more important, it is an obstacle to the attainment of the higher ends of the State.

The principle of universal suffrage, according to which all citizens legally qualified participate with equal rights of voting in the political life of the country, is bound up with the idea that this is or should be the best means of adequately satisfying the majority of individual interests; an idea which is now opposed and supplanted by the idea that the State is a self-sufficient principle; that it is not a sum, but a synthesis of individual interests and hence has its own higher and permanent ends to follow; that it is, finally, of a moral and ideal nature rather than economic and material."

It is natural that the decay of Parliament involves the need of a new form of representative government if political Democracy is to survive in those countries which are still its staunchest advocates.

But in Italy where the necessity of a perpetuation of Democracy is vigorously denied, the decay of Parliament has led to that radical transformation of the organs of the State, a transformation which is embodied in the principle that government emanates from the King and not from the people, from the Royal power and not from the Parliament.

And because the parliamentary system rests ultimately upon two main assumptions; the sovereignty of the people and the capacity of the people to delegate this sovereignty to individuals fit to legislate and govern; once these assumptions are denied and in their stead, the sovereignty of the State and the urge of the masses to be led is affirmed, Parliament loses its main reason for being the supreme organ of the State and becomes merely another medium through which the voice of the masses becomes articulate, and the nation rises to the consciousness of its problems, its aspirations and its needs.

Furthermore, where—as in the corporative State —the guild system of organization of the laboring classes of the nation rises to a position of preeminence as a political instrument of these same classes, parliament is well nigh ready to be shorn of its last vestige of authority and delegate its former power to the representatives of the corporate organization.

This is in fact what will take place in Italy, where the guilds not only take care of those functions properly inherent to them, but are going to completely supplant the old Chamber of Deputies in the part which this Chamber played in the governing machinery.

Another chapter of the pre-Fascist era is brought thus happily to its close with the doom of Parliament and the identification of Politics with the wider aspects of life.

"A State is well constituted and internally powerful when the private interests of its citizens coincide with the general interest of the State." —HEGEL.

CHAPTER VIII

THE FASCIST STATE

It is no more than a platitude to affirm that the birth of Fascism found the political world in a condition of anarchy and decadence.

The theocratic principle of the autocratic state, which derived the authority of the Sovereign from the will of God, was not only discredited but ridiculed as well.

The humanistic principle of the liberal state, which was born out of a vague belief in the worth of the individual, had seen its best days and had degenerated into chaotic and meaningless practice.

The democratic principle, which presupposes the inborn wisdom of the masses, the fundamental moral goodness and unquestioned intellectual capacity of the people, had been thoroughly disproved by the actual facts in those countries where it had been most characteristically tried.

Nothing else seemed left for mankind than the communist folly bringing the world suddenly back to the primitive state of a society of ants or bees.

Faced with this symptomatic decay of all political organizations, the first task of Fascism became that of re-establishing the faith of mankind into the State as an Ideal.

The very words "The State as an Ideal" sound rather incongruous in our modern world where a materialistic and mechanistic conception of life and the universe has reigned supreme throughout the last hundred years.

No book on the philosophy of the State published in these eventful years ever attempted to find in the State something more than an outgrowth of the original tribal group of the primitive ages.

According to modern authors on Politics, the State came into being as a natural product of the evolution of social and political organization of human society. To set the conception of the State as an Ideal to be realized, as a motive force, therefore, of the life of man, was as far from their ordinary ways of thinking as the thought that the Nation is gifted with an organic life of its own.

And, as it is impossible for man to give his allegiance to what does not partake of the soul, the State appeared as a symbol of all that there was to be feared, hated, dominated, or exploited in this world.

No wonder then that the soldier found military service unbearable, the citizen found the payment of taxes a burden, the educator found education to be a perpetual lie, the priest found that his mission conflicted with the mission of the State, and so forth and so on.

The State was, in turn, identified with the land, with the king, with the people . . . but never with the essence of the Nation, because that was equivalent to an admission of claims of a spiritual nature; claims which appeared preposterous, if not ridiculous in those blessed days when Bluckner was writing "Force and Matter" and Robert Ingersoll had taken the place of Ralph Waldo Emerson.

The reason of being of the State is not to be found instead, according to Fascism, in external causes like, for instance, a social contract of its component parts, but it is to be found in its nature of Ethical entity summing up in itself the collective expression of the Nation. Without State there is no Nation, as the Nation first rises to consciousness of itself in the State and through the State.

Were the State not an Idea, which, in the words of Gentile, "transcends all particular expressions in time, or any contingent and materialistically defined form," but simply the product of a social contract; it would remain always at the mercy of the contracting parties; all powers of directing the life of the commonwealth would not reside with the State, but with these parties.

It is, instead, the supreme characteristic of the Fascist State the capacity to will and to act, to legislate and to command, the capacity, in other words, of operating as an ethical personality.

This concept of the function that the State must fulfill in the world of man, and which represents, without doubt, one of the most original concepts of Fascism, finds its most brief and explicit expression in the definition of the State given in the Fascist Labor Charter, the Magna Carta of Fascism.

To read this definition means to read the opening of a new chapter in the development of human society; it means also to breathe again the air of Idealism coming to vivify once more the life of man into an expression of spiritual energy; it means finally to prove the sense of elation and pride derived from the realization that it is yet possible for man to know and realize some of the highest truths of the spiritual world.

"The Italian Nation is an organism which has an aim, a life, and means of action superior both in element of power and element of time, to the aims, the life and the means of action of the individuals, or groups of individuals who compose it."

Thus reads the definition of the State in the Fascist Labor Charter.

But what a slow, tortuous, painful process is hidden beneath that progress of the conception of what truly is the function of the State from its first definition to the last.

We find thus that in his first utterance on the subject, Mussolini says, on November 16, 1922:

"It is not of definite programs that Italy is lacking, no, what is lacking to Italy are men and the will to apply those programs. The State represents today this firm and determined will."

This conception of the State presupposes the existence of satisfactory programs of action and the restriction of the function of the State to that of interpreter and executor of those programs; only a very poor and inadequate function at the best.

But on the seventh of January of the following year he is a little more precise:

"The State exists for all the people, but is also above the people, and, if necessary, against the people. . . . It is against them whenever they attempt to place their particular interests above the general interests of the Nation."

On the twenty-sixth of the same month he is even more explicit:

"The National State conciliates in itself the interests of all social categories, and wants decidedly the greatness of the nation through the welfare of the single citizen."

The definition of the State finds thus an always better expression as time goes on, but the supreme function of the Fascist State: that of safeguarding and incarnating the Idea, the Essence and the Will of the Nation, is awaiting its true definition as yet.

This definition is almost at the point of being definitely uttered when Mussolini, speaking on the eighth of August, 1924, says:

". . . the State sums up in itself not only the political consciousness of the Nation at the present time, but also what the Nation is going to be in the future."

Had he gone still one step farther at that time, had he announced the essential supremacy of the State over the Nation, if the Nation is to live at all, the definition would have been practically complete.

But it is only one year later, on August 8, 1925, that he says:

"It is the purpose of Fascism to unify the Nation through the sovereign State, the State which is above all and can be against all, because it represents the moral continuity of the Nation. Without State there is no Nation."

Without State there is no Nation. These words reverse the commonly accepted principle of modern political science that without Nation there is no State. They seem at first to run counter to all evidence, but they represent, instead, for Fascism, the expression of a fundamental truth, one of those truths which are at the very basis of the social life of mankind.

To say, in fact, that in the State and through the State a Nation first rises to the consciousness of itself, means that the State gives to the people that political, social and moral unity without which there is no possibility of a true national life. Furthermore, the State is the only organ through which the anonymous will of the people can find the expression of will of a single personality, conscious of its aims, its purposes and its needs.

The State becomes thus invested with the dignity, the attributes and the power of an ethical personality which exists and lives, and develops and progresses or decays, and, finally dies.

Compared to this personality of the State with its characteristics of transcendent values and its problems of momentous magnitude, the personality of the single individual loses all of that importance which it had assumed in the modern times.

It is possible thus for a Fascist writer, G. Corso, to write:

"... the liberal idea, the democratic idea and the socialistic idea, start from the common presupposition that the individual must be free because only the individual is real. To such a conception Fascism opposes the other that the individual is to be considered as a highly transitory and apparent thing, when compared to the ethnic reality of the race, the spiritual reality of the Nation, the ethical reality of the State."

Or for Mussolini to state:

"... Liberalism denied the State in the interest of the particular individual; Fascism, instead reaffirms the State as the true reality of the individual."

In this shifting of emphasis from the individual to the State, the very functions of the one become part of the life of the other. The State must, therefore, concern itself not only with social order, political organization and economic problems, but with morality and religion as well.

The Fascist State is, in other words, not only the social, political and economic organization of the people of one nation, but is also the outward manifestation of their moral and religious life, and, as such, is therefore an Ethical State.

The Fascist State presupposes that man beside being an individual is also a social being, and therefore, willing and compelled to come under some form of disciplinary authority for the good of the whole.

It presupposes also that the highest law for man is the moral law, and that right or wrong, good or evil, have well defined meanings in this moral law and are beyond the pale of individual likes or dislikes or individual judgment.

It presupposes, finally, that the Nation-State is gifted with an organic life of its own, which far transcends in meaning the life of the individual, and whose development, growth and progress, follow laws which man cannot ignore or modify, but only discover and obey.

Henceforth the State is no longer a word denoting the authority underlying a complex system of relationships between individuals, classes, organizations, etc., but something of far greater import, far greater meaning than that: it is a living entity, it is the highest spiritual entity of the political world.

In the words of Giovanni Gentile:

"We affirm our belief that the State is not a system of hindrances and external juridical controls from which men flee, but an ethical being, which, like the conscience of the individual, manifests its personality and achieves its historical growth in human society. Thus it is conscious of not being hedged in by special limits, but of being open, ready, and capable of expanding as a collective and yet individual will.

"The Nation is that will, conscious of itself and of its own historical past, which, as we formulate it in our minds, defines and delineates our nationality, generating an end to be attained, a mission to be realized. For that will, in case of need, our lives are sacrificed, for our lives are genuine, worthy and endowed with incontestable value only as they are spent in the accomplishment of that mission.

"The State's active and dynamic consciousness is a system of thought, of ideas, of interests to be satisfied and of morality to be realized. Hence the State is, as it ought to be, a teacher; it maintains and develops schools to promote this morality. In the school the State comes to a consciousness of its real being."

And, in the words of Alfredo Rocco, ex-minister of Justice:

"The Nation is that living, moral entity, which, although composed of individuals, transcends the scope and life of its components, identifying itself with the history and the finalities of an uninterrupted series of generations.

"The Nation is a moral entity, since it is composed of human beings; for man is not only matter, and the purpose of man's life, far from being the materialistic one of all animal life, is rather a spiritual one peculiar to man and to man alone, and is a purpose which every form of human society strives to attain as well as its stage of development will allow it.

"The Nation is an entity with a unity brought about by common traditions among the people that compose it, traditions formed in the course of time owing to the working of a variety of influences, such as community of

123

topographical and climatic conditions; community of language, race, culture, religion, laws, customs, history, feelings and volitions; community also of economic interests and territory having clearly marked geographical boundaries."

According to these views of Fascist thinkers the State is, therefore, no more a purely abstract political entity, but a concrete being whose growth, development and progress follow laws of their own; and the Nation is, at the same time, the material substance and the spiritual essence of the State. The process of education implies, thus, primarily, the formation and the fostering of the national consciousness.

Within the framework of the national Ideal, man is capable, in fact, to rise to the perception and to bring about the realization of some of the highest truths of the spiritual world. And that it is so, should not prove entirely surprising when we stop to consider that it is an inherent condition of the fundamental nature of man that of parcelling out what falls under the domain of sense experience; that of apprehending separately what could never be comprehended in its primary indissoluble unity.

It is a historical truism that throughout the long struggle for mastery of the world within and the world without, man has found always necessary, if he wanted to bring any form of order out of the surrounding chaos, to circumscribe and delimit the whole of reality.

We see this process applied in the scientific field, where the scientist does not attempt to undertake the study of nature as a whole, but limits himself to much humbler tasks; in the artistic field where the artist does not attempt to seize all of life in its essential unity, but remains satisfied with the portrayal of those particular aspects of life which fall within the domain of his individual sensibility; in the field of religion where the priest does not attempt to understand God as God, but seeks to comprehend His essence as a sublimation of the essence of man; and in the political field, where man arrives, by successive stages, to the conception and realization of the national ideal. In itself this ideal is no more than a transitory stage to something still fuller, still greater yet to come, but it represents, for the time being, that expression of political organization vivified the most largely by the spiritual element in man.

One of the primary causes of the decline of the western world must be, thus, inevitably ascribed to the rapidly declining belief in national ideals, and in their substitution with personal aims and individual gains. The realization of those ideals requires the sacrifice of these very aims and gains, or, at any rate, their subjection and their restriction within well defined limits—limits which have become, with the passing of time, more and more incompatible with the spread and triumph of Individualism.

To bring mankind back to the true vision of the relative worth of the individual and of the nation, that organism of which the single individual is an integral, although accidental and infinitesimal part, needs a truly superhuman effort.

Gone is forever the time when it was possible

to find a way to the heart of man through his devotion to higher things than his personal affairs; gone is the time when it was possible to appeal to the mystic side of his nature through a religious commandment; gone, finally, is the time when it was possible to illuminate the reasoning powers of his mind with the light of ideals whose existence and whose reason of being cannot be proved through the powers of reason.

All that remains is an appeal to force, to compulsion; intellectual as well as physical, an appeal to what lies outside of man, to what he fears and with what he must of necessity abide.

Such a forceful appeal is made at present by Fascism which, compelling the elder or educating the younger, is slowly but surely bringing the Italian people to the comprehension of the worth, the beauty and the significance of the National Ideal.

But if the Fascist State is an Ethical State, it is also, and above all, a Sovereign State. Its power, therefore, is not conditional to the will of the people, the parliament, the King, or any other of its constituent elements: it is rather immanent in its very essence.

Once more we find Individualism with its offsprings: the liberal, democratic and radical doctrines, in antithetic contrast to Fascism on an issue of paramount importance for the whole world of man.

Passing from the Liberal doctrine, which had conceded the sovereignty of the State to the people as a whole, to the democratic doctrine, which this sovereignty gave away to the numerical majority and to the socialistic, communistic doctrine which invested it in one small particular class, we find an always greater abdication of the soverign attributes to an always more restricted constituent element of the nation.

To affirm instead, as Fascism does, that "All is in the State and for the State; nothing outside the State, nothing against the State," means to affirm that the Ideal State is the one which is above individuals, organizations, castes or classes; or above all particularized interests, needs or ambitions.

The rise of Fascism destroys forever, thus, that Gordian Knot of apparently insoluble social problems born from the clash of conflicting interests of individuals within the State. It destroys also the subjection of the welfare of the State to the welfare of any individual, or any group of individuals, or even the totality of all the people. And, as the resort to the Will of God as final authority in all matters which may affect the welfare of the State has lost all meaning in our modern, individualistic, materialistic Society, in the same way the demagogic appeal to the will of the people is to lose all significance in the coming Fascist Society.

The triumph of Fascism means, in fact, that the role of the people is finally brought back to that secondary importance which it assumes when considered in its proper relation to the other elements of the Nation-State.

The place, therefore, which the People occupy in the social order as conceived by Liberalism is, in the new scheme of things planned by Fascism, taken actually by the Nation-State; that entity of which the People remain still the basic part, but which comprehends it and transcends it both in absolute meaning and in ultimate value.

"Anti-individualistic, the Fascist conception of life," says Mussolini, "stresses the importance of the State and accepts the individual only insofar as his interests coincide with those of the State, which stands for the conscience and the universal will of man as historic entity.

"The Fascist conception of life is opposed to classical liberalism which arose as a reaction to absolutism and exhausted its historical function when the State became the expression of the conscience and the will of the people.

"Liberalism denied the State in the name of the individual; Fascism reasserts the rights of the State as expressing the real essence of the individual. And if liberty is to be the attribute of living men and not of abstract dummies invented by individualistic liberalism, then Fascism stands for liberty, and for the only liberty worth having, the liberty of the State and of the individual within the State.

"The Fascist conception of the State is all-embracing; outside of it no human or spiritual values can exist. Thus understood, Fascism is totalitarian and the Fascist State—a synthesis and a unit inclusive of all values—interprets, develops and potentiates the whole life of a people.

"No individuals or groups (political parties, cultural associations, economic unions, social classes) are outside the State. Fascism is therefore opposed to Socialism, to which unity within the State (as an amalgamation of classes into a single economic and ethical reality) is unknown; which sees in history nothing but class struggle.

"Fascism is likewise opposed to trade-unionism as a class weapon. But when brought within the orbit of the State, Fascism recognizes the real needs which gave rise to socialism and trade-unionism, giving them due weight in the guild or corporative system in which divergent interests are coordinated and harmonized within the unity of the State.

"Grouped according to their several interests, individuals form classes; they form trade-unions when organized according to their several economic activities; but first and foremost they form the State, which must never be considered as a mere matter of numbers, as simply the sum of the individuals forming the majority.

"Fascism is therefore opposed to that form of democracy which equates a nation to the majority, lowering it to the level of the largest number; but it is the purest form of democracy if the nation be considered—as it should be—from the point of view of quality rather than quantity, as an Idea, the mightiest because the most ethical; the most coherent, the truest; expressing itself in a people as the conscience and will of the few—if not, indeed, of one; and ending to express itself in the conscience and the will of the mass, of the whole group ethnically moulded by natural and historical conditions into a nation advancing, as one conscience and one will, along the same line of development and spiritual formation. A nation is not a race, nor a geographically defined region, but a people historically perpetuating itself: a multitude unified by an idea and imbued with the will to live, the will to power, self-consciousness, personality.

"Insofar as it is embodied in a State, this higher

personality becomes a nation. It is not the nation which generates the State; that is an antiquated naturalistic concept which afforded a basis for nineteenth century publicity in favor of national governments. Rather, it is the State which creates the nation, conferring volition and therefore real life on a people made aware of their moral unity.

"The right to national independence does not arise from any merely literary and idealistic form of self-consciousness; still less from a more or less passive and unconscious de facto situation, but from an active, self-conscious, political will expressing itself in action and ready to prove its rights. It arises, in short, from the existence, at least in fieri, of a State. Indeed, it is the State which, as the expression of a universal ethical will, creates the right to national independence.

"A nation, as expressed in the State, is a living, ethical entity only insofar as it is progressive. Inactivity is death. Therefore the State is not only Authority which governs and confers legal form and spiritual value on individual wills, but it is also Power which makes its will felt and respected beyond its own frontiers, thus affording practical proof of the universal character of the decisions necessary to ensure its development. This implies organization and expansion, potential if not actual. Thus the State equates itself to the will of man, whose development cannot be checked by obstacles and which, by achieving self-expression, demonstrates its own infinity.

"The Fascist State, as a higher and more powerful expression of personality, is a force, but a spiritual one. It sums up all the manifestations of the moral and intellectual life of man. Its functions cannot therefore be limited to those of enforcing order and keeping the peace, as the liberal doctrine had it. It is no mere mechanical device for defining the sphere within which the individual may duly exercise his supposed rights. The Fascist State is an inwardly accepted standard and rule of conduct, a discipline of the whole person; it permeates the will no less than the intellect. It stands for a principle which becomes the central motive of man as a member of civilized society, sinking deep down into his personality; it dwells in the heart of the man of action and of the thinker, of the artist and of the man of science: soul of the soul.

"Fascism, in short, is not only a law-giver and a founder of institutions, but an educator and promoter of spiritual life. It aims at refashioning not only the forms of life but their content—man, his character and his faith. To achieve this purpose it enforces discipline and uses authority, entering into the soul and ruling with undisputed sway. Therefore it has chosen as its emblem the Lictor's rods, the symbol of unity, strength and justice."

Arrived thus at the end of our rapid survey of the Fascist State, we find ourselves facing the inescapable fact that the philosophy of Fascism, with its idealistic conceptions of the Ethical State as a spiritual entity, and of the Nation-State as a thing of supreme worth in the life of man, rises far above the philosophy of Individualism as the true answer to the social needs of this life.

"Men have failed to understand what it means to have the strongest, richest and noblest nature invested with supreme powers." —BRANDES.

CHAPTER IX

THE CONSTITUTION OF THE FASCIST STATE

It has been said: "Fascism is Dictatorship and Dictatorship is Fascism—Fascism is therefore anathema and ought to be ostracized."

But is Dictatorship synonimous with Fascism, and is the Fascist form of government truly a Dictatorship?

May it not be instead that Dictatorship is not an element of Fascism at all, and that Fascism is firmly opposed to all forms of Dictatorship, political as well as otherwise?

Let us get acquainted, therefore, with the organization of the Fascist State and find out for ourselves how much truth there is in this so generalized and yet so highly mistaken notion.

To begin with, the Fascist State being a Sovereign State, must of necessity emphasize the authority of that organ of government which best typifies the attributes of sovereignty.

We find thus the executive branch of government strengthened at the expense of the legislative one which, in the Italian form of liberal state, had become a veritable monster devouring all initiative, all originality.

In the Fascist State the legislative power belongs both to the Parliament and to the King, who through his Secretary of State, exercises the legislative power by refusing to let any bill which he disapproves of receive parliamentary consideration.

Furthermore, it is in the faculty of the executive power to emanate juridical norms without the immediate consent of the legislative branch of government, whenever the supreme good of the State may require it.

This new power of the executive sets well defined limits to the activity of the legislators, bringing this activity back to that true function of legislation so often misinterpreted in the degeneration of the liberal-democratic doctrines.

Having denied the sovereignty of the people, Fascism holds that the branch of legislature elected by popular vote, which represented both the symbol and the depositary of this sovereignty in the Liberal State, loses practically all its previous importance and becomes simply a consultive organ whose proper function is collaboration with the other powers of the State.

And, as this collaboration is realized in the best possible way, when, during the discussion of each law, specialized knowledge is brought to bear on each specific problem, it becomes necessary that the Chamber of Deputies be transformed from a political congregation of heterogeneous individuals to a specialized homogeneous body of experts on the various aspects of life.

Finally, having taken away from the masses the privilege of choosing as their representatives people who could be interpreters of their political ideas, Fascism gives back to the masses the right of choosing as their representatives persons who can safeguard and protect their professional interests.

The Chamber of Deputies becomes thus a vocational Chamber whose four hundred members are elected by lists drawn up by the Fascist Grand Council containing one thousand names designated by the various vocational groups of the nation.

Parliament, in the Fascist State, is then nothing more than a voice of the true creative and productive forces of the nation, and provides no echo for outbursts of political passion.

Another element contributing to the strengthening of the executive power is brought about by the change of that time-honored tradition of the Liberal State: the responsibility of the Ministers toward the Parliament.

In the Fascist State the Ministers are responsible only to their Premier, who, in turn, is responsible to the King alone and to no other.

This new state of things puts an end to that dependency of the ministerial function upon the political fortune of the Ministers, assuring thus the very stability and continuity of the government. It represents also the abrogation of the main postulate of the Liberal State: the postulate that the Executive and the Legislative functions must be kept always separated in the perfect type of government.

Above all, foundation and mainstay of the Fascist reform is the theory that all powers of the State belong to the King who personifies the very authority of the State, and that he simply delegates the executive, legislative and judiciary functions to the various organs of the State.

The King, in other words, not the People, is the true Sovereign of the Fascist State.

Highly characteristic of this reform is therefore the place which Fascism assigns to the Premier, who is also Secretary of State as well as Head of the Government; inferior in authority only to the King, and invested with a dignity and a responsibility far superior to that of any other organ of the state.

This high station assigned by the Fascist reform to the Head of the Government is based in the last analysis upon the idealistic conception of the hierarchy of human values constituted by the people of a nation and, therefore, of an hierarchy of human dignities which proceed by successive steps from the lowest person to the highest.

According to this idealistic conception it is only proper and fitting that, at the supreme pinnacle of this hierarchical arrangement of society, should be placed the Head of the Government, who, while proceeding from the People and being part of the People, nevertheless represents the King, who neither proceeds from the People nor is part of the People.

This authority conferred to the Head of the Government is far from making of him what is commonly meant today by the word "Dictator."

Time it was when a dictator was a person elected

by the People and to whom the People delegated their authority for a determinate period of time only. A dictator was then servant, not master of the People; he worked in the interest of the People only and, inasmuch as the People were then identified with the State, he worked in the interest of the State.

In our times, instead, a dictator is he who stands opposite to the People and in contrast to the People as the Power which is the State, and that this Power is able to exercise as he sees fit or believes right, in the interest of the People or against the interest of the People, and not necessarily for the good of the State.

For this type of personage there is no room in the Fascist State. The two poles of the Fascist State are the People and the King, not the People and the Head of the Government. While the King personifies the sovereign authority of the State, authority which in itself sums up all powers: executive, legislative and judiciary, the Head of the Government represents only the King in his relationship with the People.

It is thus that in the Fascist reform of the State, the King is still the only one who has the right to declare war or to accept peace, the right of pardoning those condemned by the judiciary organs of the State, the right of stipulating in the name of the State, treaties of alliance with other states and, finally, the right to be outside and above all laws.

Had not the liberal doctrine constituting the foundation of the modern democratic forms of government brought about a dangerous shift of authority from the King to the People by investing the latter with the power which properly belongs to the former, we would never have witnessed, perhaps, this Fascist effort of curbing the legislative function of the People's representatives.

As it is, instead, through the increase of prestige and authority of the Head of the Government, the restrictions of the powers of the legislative branch and the participation of the executive in the legislative activity, Fascism has succeeded very well in the necessary task of strengthening the central power of the State without, for that matter, making possible the rise of any dictatorship in its government organization.

The only imponderable element which remains now and will remain forever, of course, is the personality of the Head of the Government, which may have such heroic qualities as to shadow all other elements of the State combined. In such cases, as the present one, the danger may arise that the world shall mistake him for a Dictator, or, what the man in the street believes to be a tyrant.

But such cases are not likely to happen very often in the history of a nation. And then . . . a hero can very well afford to be mistaken for a tyrant. Time is the father of justice, and "to the generous and true, harbinger of Glory is always Death."

The description of the Fascist reform would not be complete without mentioning the part played by the "Gran Consiglio" of the Fascist party. This Grand Council is an absolutely new organ of government, a purely Fascist creation, which finds no counterpart in the constitution of any other state.

The Grand Council, being the voice of the only recognized political party of the nation: the Fascist party, in the absence of a political Chamber of Deputies, is the only recognized political organ of the Fascist State.

It stands also between the People and the Government as interpreter of the one and adviser of the other; finally, it is the depositary of the power of Fascism within the Fascist State.

The Grand Council does not legislate nor pass judgment, neither enforces laws nor repeals them. What it does accomplish is something of a very elusive character; it maintains always alive the Fascist tradition.

Its more specific functions are: the approval of the King's successor; the designation to the Crown of the Head of the Government and of the Ministers; the choice of the names to be submitted to the various vocational groups for the election of their deputies; the discussion of all questions which may affect the constitution of the Fascist State and the deliberation of all issues which may affect the life of the Fascist party.

In brief, the Grand Council is not the Crown, not the People, not the Government, not the Party; it is simply the organ through which Fascism will perpetuate itself in the Italian nation as long as there are Italians fit to become Fascists.

Having brought about its momentuous reform of government, Fascism assumes the other arduous task of renewing the whole administrative structure of the State. This renewal is accomplished by destroying once and forever the notion of the Liberal-Democratic doctrine that local authority depends upon the local expression of the numerical majority of the sovereign people and substituting for it the conception that local authority, as well as all authority, derives from a common source: the executive power, which is above all local prejudices, ambitions or interests.

The elective Mayor is thus replaced by a "Podestá" nominated by the executive, responsible for his acts not to the People but to the Head of the Government.

In this new system, local struggles, ambitions and interests cannot influence any longer the orderly procedure of the law which must concern itself with the regulation of the communal life. Gone are thus forever all hopes of personal aggrandizement of individuals or groups obtained through political favors at the expense of the commonwealth. What the individual has lost, the community has gained, and the gain offsets the loss by far. And as the authority of the head of the commune — the basic nucleus of social life — has been strengthened, in the same way the authority of the provincial representative of the executive power, the "Prefetto" of a province, has received by Fascism a new and higher confirmation. The communal and provincial life must henceforth develop within iron-bound limits of order and discipline which the individual must recognize and obey.

Resuming, then, we find that the highest achievement of the Fascist reform consists in having shorn the People of all power and in having conferred this power to a central organ which in turn delegates its authority to secondary and derivative organs of control and direction of the national life.

The true essence of the Fascist Constitution of

the State lies thus with the derivation of authority from above rather than from below; from the King rather than from the People; and with the centralization of powers within that executive organ of which the King is the ideal, even if only apparent, personification.

CHAPTER X

THE CORPORATIVE IDEA

To understand the reasons for the debacle of the economic life of modern capitalistic states, it will be sufficient to review the fundamental conceptions underlying their economic practice. Only by getting at the roots of the tree shall we ever be able to find out the cause of the decay of its branches.

Those conceptions can be briefly summarized thus:

1. The economic life of man is a field of action which can be abstracted and separated from all other fields of action of his spiritual activity.

2. The economic life of man is determined only by materialistic factors.

3. Economic progress can derive only from the free play of human egoisms and human ambitions.

4. Private, individual interests, are the only moving forces of all economic initiatives.

5. Increase of wealth can derive only from open competition.

6. The wealth of a community can be measured in terms of the riches of single individuals.

7. The only proper function of the State in the economic life of a nation can be summed up by the formula: Laissez-Faire, a formula devised by the liberal school but fostering only the interests of a reactionary class.

8. The war of classes is a natural phenomenon and is unavoidable. The important thing in this war, as in all wars, is for those in power to retain, and if possible, to assert this power even more forcefully.

9. Production of goods is the main function in the economic life of a nation, and increase of production the only desirable aim. It is assumed that distribution of these goods will take care of itself somehow in a mysterious but infallible way and will adjust itself invariably to conditions, according to the working of such empiric laws as for instance, the law of supply and demand.

10. Private wealth, obtained by the individual in any amount and through any device he has seen fit to use, is sacred and inviolable.

Belief in this decalogue and practice of its commandments have brought modern capitalist states to the present condition of chaos and despair, when they must acknowledge that the communist propaganda has become for the first time a real menace to their social structure.

What does communism do in effect?

Accepting the tenet that class struggle is unavoidable, communism takes up the challenge of capitalism and brings this struggle to its final issue:

the triumph of one class: the proletarian class, at the expense of all other classes.

Accepting the tenet that the State is an organ devoid of transcendent significance, communism makes of the State simply a tool for furthering the private interests of the individual.

Finally, accepting the tenet that materialist interests are the only motive forces of the life of man, communism enthrones them as new gods to serve and worship and if necessary, to die for.

Communism, in other words, born out of capitalism, can succeed only, and is actually succeeding, by emphasizing those diseases which gnaw at the very heart of the capitalistic system.

Communism, strange as it may seem, is thus nothing more than economic individualism carried to its logical and fatal conclusion.

Fascism, which is the very antithesis of Individualism, stands as the nemesis of all economic doctrines and all economic practice of both the capitalistic and the communistic systems. Fascism holds that:

1. The economic life of man cannot be abstracted and separated from the whole of his spiritual life. In the words of Mussolini: "The economic man does not exist. Man is integral; he is political, economic, religious, saint and warrior at the same time."

2. The economic life of man is influenced, if not actually determined, by idealistic factors.

3. True economic progress can derive only from the concerted effort of individuals who know how to sacrifice their personal egoism and ambitions for the good of the whole.

4. Economic initiatives cannot be left to the arbitrary decisions of private, individual interests.

5. Open competition, if not wisely directed and restricted, actually destroys wealth instead of creating it.

6. The wealth of a community is something intangible which cannot be identified with the sum of riches of single individuals.

7. The proper function of the State in the Fascist system is that of supervising, regulating and arbitrating the relationships of capital and labor, employers and employees, individuals and associations, private interests and national interests.

8. Class war is avoidable and must be avoided. Class war is deleterious to the orderly and fruitful life of the nation, therefore it has no place in the Fascist State.

9. More important than the production of wealth is its right distribution, distribution which must benefit in the best possible way all the classes of the nation, hence, the nation itself.

10. Private wealth belongs not only to the individual, but, in a symbolic sense, to the State as well.

These fundamental tenets of Fascist economy derive in turn from those basic conceptions of the Fascist doctrine of the State which we have expounded in the chapter of the "Fascist State." We have said there, in fact, that the Fascist State is a Sovereign State. This means that there cannot be any single economic interests which are above the general economic interests of the State, no individual, economic initiatives which do not fall under the supervision and regulation of the State, no relationships of the various classes of the nation which are not the concern of the State.

Furthermore, the Fascist State is an Ethical State. This means that all the factors influencing the life of a nation: the economic, the social, the political, etc., are brought into the Fascist State under the dominion of the moral law, which becomes not only the supreme law of the individual, but the supreme law of the State as well.

"One invisible tie binds together all the people of a nation. There cannot be any joy or any pain experienced by one single individual which shall not ultimately affect the welfare of the whole nation."

This is the principle of Fascist Ethics which, translated and applied to the realm of Economics, has transformed the economic organization of the State.

If it is true that one invisible tie binds together the destinties of all the people of one nation, then it is also true that the terms wealthy and pauper, capitalist and worker, landowner and farmer, employer and employee, lose their antagonistic meaning altogether and remain to signify brethren in spirit if not in flesh, engaged from different angles, on different planes, in the arduous task of building up a nation's life.

We see thus the Fascist State resolutely enter the economic field to dictate what shall be from now on the relationship between capital and labor, employer and employee, landowner and farmhand, industrialist and worker.

147

This relationship meant, up to the rise of Fascism, only and simply class war. But—

". . . Class war," Mussolini said on Jan. 2, 1923, "cannot be more than a transitory episode of the life of a people. It cannot be a daily phenomenon, because it would mean in the end the destruction of all wealth."

And speaking on the 20th of December, 1923, Mussolini said:

". . . The mistake of Marxism is that of believing that a nation is made of two classes only. A mistake even greater is that of believing that these two classes are in a perpetual state of war. There may be, it is true, contrast of interests, but it cannot be more than transitory; it can never be systematic. This systematic antithesis, which has furnished the basis for all socialistic theories, is not a fact but an assumption. Its place has to be taken by collaboration."

Finally, in his definition of the doctrine of Fascism, Mussolini has stated once and for all the terms of the Fascist reaction to the war of classes within the State:

"Having denied historic materialism, which sees in man mere puppets on the surface of history, appearing and disappearing on the crest of the waves, while the real, directing forces move and work in the depths, Fascism also denies the immutable and irreparable character of the class struggle which is the natural outcome of this economic conception of history."

But the war of classes is not the only problem left unsolved by the liberal or the democratic State. There is another equally important problem left without solution: the problem of adequate production and efficient distribution. Of the aspect of this problem, Mussolini said on June 2, 1923:

"The collaboration between the one who furnishes the brow and the one who supplies the brains; the organization of all the elements of production in hierarchies unavoidable and necessary; this is the program through the realization of which it is possible for the people to attain material welfare and for the nation to attain prosperity and power."

These last words are the key to the attitude of Fascism toward the facts of production and distribution.

Knowing that the social problem cannot be entirely solved by regulation of the rapports between capital and labor, but must be solved also with regard to the general facts of production and distribution, Fascism decrees that the productive forces of the nation cannot be any longer at the mercy of the individual's selfishness and greed, but must be brought, instead, under the supreme discipline of the State.

By delimiting thus the field of action of capital and labor, by harmonizing production and distribution to the actual needs of the nation, the legislation of Fascism has accomplished in the realm of

Economics what no legislation of any other political system has ever been able to accomplish; namely, a co-ordination of all the economic forces of the nation so that the material life of the people may be free of struggles, strikes, unemployment, class war, concentrated wealth and widespread misery.

To bring about such a magic transformation of the economic life of the nation, Fascism has made use of the most characteristic phenomenon of the modern era: the syndicalist phenomenon. Originated as an instrument of the war of classes, syndicalism attempted to organize the various categories of workers in syndical organizations having no other goal than the protection of the material welfare of their own members. These organizations were devoted thus to the furthering of supremely particularized interests, ready to set themselves against each other and against the State itself, whenever those interests were menaced or conflicted with others.

The problem which presented itself as an ominous menace upon the horizon of Fascism at the outset of its very life in Italy was, therefore, to bring at once the phenomenon of syndicalism under the authority of the State, and, successively, to transform its original aim of protecting the interests of the proletariat into protecting the interests of the whole nation.

This could be accomplished only by enlarging the narrow form of the original syndicalist organizations into larger forms which would include all the citizens of the nation into an all-comprehensive national manifestation. This manifestation of the Italians of all classes, all professions, all trades and all creeds into the framework of one enormous and far-reaching organization, which has for its end the material welfare of the whole, is called National Syndicalism.

This National Syndicalism represents the first attempt made to bring the egotistic claims of the individual under the discipline of the Sovereign State; for the realization of an aim which transcends the welfare of the individual and identifies itself with the prosperity of the whole nation.

To make this discipline possible, and the sovereignty effective in practice as well as in theory, Fascism has devised the "Corporazione," an instrument of social life destined to exercise the most far-reaching influence upon the economic development of Fascist States. (The Italian word "Corporazione" which is currently translated into English by the apparently analogous word "Corporation," means, more exactly in the Italian language, what the word "Guild" means in English; that is: associations of persons engaged in kindred pursuits. We shall nevertheless follow the general usage to obviate the danger of misunderstandings.)

Within the Corporations the interests of producers and consumers, employers and employees, individuals and associations are interlocked and integrated in a unique and univocal way, while all types of interests are brought under the aegis of the State.

Finally, through these corporations the State may at any time that it deems fit, or that the need requires, intervene within the economic life of the individual to let the supreme interests of the nation have precedence over his private, particular interests, even to the point where his work, his savings, his whole fortune may need be pledged, and if absolutely necessary, sacrificed.

The essential difference existing between syndical organizations and corporations can best be illustrated by the comparison of the function they fulfill.

> "While the recognized syndical organization," says G. Bottai, "are juridical personalities of public character, the corporations, instead, are organs of administration of the State. It happens thus that while the syndical function is strictly a prerogative of the Syndicates; the corporative function is uniquely of the domain of the State. . . ."

The Fascist State can be defined then as a "State of Syndical composition and corporative function."

Through these corporations the Fascist State not only recognizes the specific interests of individuals, of classes and categories—also recognized by the liberal and the democratic State—but, in addition, organizes them, submits them to the authority and the discipline of the State and makes of them the most appropriate instruments for the development of the economic life of the nation.

This social reform, which was implicit in the first recognition of syndicalist associations in France with the law of March 21, 1884, ends forever the neutral position of the Liberal and the Democratic State in the conflicts arising from clashes of opposing interests of the different classes.

> "All modern history," says G. Bottai, "that is all contemporaneous life, leads to the cor-

porative conception of the State, with the inclusion of Economics within the State or the
identification of Economics with Politics."
And Mussolini:

"Fascism answers today the requirements of
universal character. It resolves in effect the
threefold problem of the relationships between
the State and the individual, between the State
and the various groups and between the groups
which are organized and those which are not."

Fifty long, dreary years of struggles, strikes, civil
wars, anarchy and depressions, were necessary to
bring about the Fascist reform, but, finally, a new
day has dawned for mankind: a day in which the
haphazard development of the syndicalist phenomenon, which is the necessary and inevitable result of our industrial development, is at last directed
toward a well defined goal and constrained within
the boundaries set by the discipline and the authority of the State.

To have brought about such magnificent progress in the economic organization of a nation is
undoubtedly an achievement of supreme worth,
but the originality of the Fascist conception of the
corporative state is not exhausted by such an
achievement. We must never lose sight of the fact
that, as Fascism is more than a corporative system,
so corporative principle is something more than a
mere principle of economics. And, properly, in
the words of another Fascist thinker, B. Donati:

"The corporative principle is a principle
vivifying the individual and the collective conduct of life; is an issue at the same time Ethical

and Social; is, finally, a need of life itself evolving and transforming in the process of time."

"In the Corporative State," Mussolini said, "the workers are placed on the same level of their employers, with the same rights and the same duties. But all the categories of life, not only workers and employers, have their assigned place within the Corporative State. It happens thus that the elements of production: capital and technique of work—which were once outside the sphere of influence or interest of the political state, find in it the best defense of their supreme interest."

And again, defining still more explicitly, still more forcefully, the Fascist Corporative State, he said:

"A whole people, a whole nation, is constituted through the corporative principle in a compact bloc of political, economical and moral energies and rises, in the Fascist State, to the dignity of an operant subject, having a will and conscious of its own destiny."

The corporative principle which is essentially an anti-individualistic princple, becomes thus the true foundation of the anti-individualistic Fascist State.

That organization to which it gives origin in the field of economics, finds its counterpart in the political field where it gives birth to a new and entirely original social formation.

This is possible because the corporative principle is, in the words of Bottai:

". . . a principle of political-juridical organization, and at the same time, a principle of social life. To give value and to organize the economic categories, to set them in a certain form of hierarchy at whose vertex is the national interest, means, at the same time, to devise not only the special organs which must realize them, but to devise a whole series or principles of subordination of two kinds: political, that is of interests and facts; juridical, that is of rights and laws. And, inasmuch as the parties of the social relationship are always two: the individual and the commonwealth; and, inasmuch as every political or juridical organization is at bottom only a system of relationships among the various individuals and between the single individual and society, it follows that the corporative principle is a principle of complex and progressive subordination of the Individual's economic interests to the greater interests of the various economic categories and the general all-comprehensive national economy."

Whoever thinks of Fascist Economy must think of it, therefore, as of something more than a new form of Economics, because it is first of all, and above all, a translation of Ethics into Economics, an application of Ethical principles to economic facts.

Whenever an ethical issue arises in the Fascist State, like the right to strike, for instance, all considerations of material interests must have, and will have, no influence on the right solution of that issue.

The ideal of economic justice is interpreted and

applied in the light shed by the Moral ideal, which, as Fascism maintains, must remain paramount in the world of man.

If Corporativism has been adopted thus for the solution of the age-old conflict between the workers and those who provide them with work, it is not entirely because of the material benefits to be expected from it, but also because of the infinite good that this principle has done in bringing about the disappearance of fratricidal struggle within the nation and in contributing toward the formation of the unitary, totalitary, integral State.

If today the corporative principle seems to answer exactly to the need of the hour, it may also happen that tomorrow another principle, another system, may better answer the same purpose.

As Balbino Giuliano says:

"Fascism holds that the Corporative system is a useful instrument which the Fascist State has devised to bring about the harmonious development of energies within the economic life of the nation and to facilitate the progress of individual activities and the increase of production. But if the function of the corporative organs may at any time become cause for regress of such activities and decrease of production, then the Fascist State will let the individual energies find for themselves, through new trials and new struggles, a new order and a new system."

In that case Corporativism will have run its course and will become a thing of the past, because if Fascism means Corporativism at present, the reverse is not true: Fascism being more than an economic system, it is also more than a political dictatorship, or more than a social revolt brought about by the affirmation of the middle class.

Each of these characteristics of the various aspects of Fascism, which various writers have erroneously believed to be its determining factor, and have been accepted from time to time as the single keynote of studies of Fascism, must be instead, brought back to their position of relative importance and integrated into the comprehensive view of Fascism as a whole philosophy of life, whose significance transcends all superficial and partial explanation.

It happens thus that economic values like industry, agriculture, commerce, etc., which are the paramount values of modern liberal and democratic form of States, are shifted, in the Fascist form of State, to subordinate positions; and properly, subordinate to those spiritual values as Religion or Fatherland, intellectual values, as Science, Education or Culture, social values, as the Family, the Race, etc.

In this way, that fictitious abstraction which was the "Homo aeconomicus" has received by the Fascist theory of the state a final, deadly blow. In its place the Ideal Man as a full human being with his aspirations and his dreams, his hopes and his fears, his possibilities and his limitations, has found anew in Fascism his voice and his expression.

Throughout all the utterances of Mussolini it is possible to perceive the paramount preoccupation of giving sensible form to the central aspiration of Fascism, the aspiration of re-establishing the furtherance of the full life of the spirit in the world of man.

Once the economic problem has been disposed of, there still remains to be solved the problem of a satisfactory human life. Economic security cannot be more than the gateway to the life of the spirit; material welfare can never be exchanged or bartered for the welfare of the soul. The Fascist Doctrine avails itself of the economic principles of syndicalism and corporation, but considers them only as a tool; its aim is not to establish the paradise of communism in which each man shall have equal share of all the good things of life, or the paradise of individualism in which each man shall have *all he can get* of the good things of life and remain satisfied with them, but to establish a state of society where man, free of the struggle for existence, may devote his energies to the greater aim of concerning himself with those things which . . . "outlast the centuries and partake of the truth."

"There is no other movement, be it spiritual or political, which has a more stable and determined doctrine than the doctrine of Fascism," Mussolini said on March 24, 1924, "We have some truths and some well defined realities before us and they are: the State, which must be above everything and everybody; the Government, which must know how to defend itself and how to defend the nation from all the attacks tending to disrupt the national life; the collaboration of the various classes, the respect of religion, the exaltation of all the national energies. The doctrine of Fascism is a doctrine of Life, and not a doctrine of death.

"Fascism rejects the economic interpretation of felicity as something to be secured socialistically, almost automatically, at a given stage of economic evolution when all will be assured of the maximum degree of comfort.

"Fascism denies the equation: Well-being equals happiness, which would make of men mere animals, thinking only how they can satiate and fatten themselves, reducing them, therefore, to a vegetative existence pure and simple. . . . And if it is true that matter has been worshipped throughout a whole century, it is also true that it is the spirit which today has taken its place."

Utterances of this type prove definitely that one of the noblest kinds of Idealism has made its appearance in our midst, and, although still greatly misunderstood and vilipended today, will not fail to bring tomorrow a renewal of our innner and outer forms of life.

The whole constitution of Fascism is permeated by the spirit of its idealistic doctrine: the ripartition of powers, the role of the hierarchy, the basis of law, the relationship with the Church, the organization of the family; all the elements of the Fascist State reflect the light of this new Idealism taking the place of Positivism, Materialism, Pragmatism and all other doctrines which are the negation of the eternal urge of Man toward the good life.

CHAPTER XI

THE CORPORATIVE SYSTEM

A gradual and progressive unfoldment of Fascist practice and theory, testifying to the truth that
Fascism is still in the making because the Fascist
revolution is far from being an accomplished fact,
is reflected in the various steps through which proletarian syndicalism becomes National syndicalism,
Corporative system and, finally, State organization.

The first step is constituted by the law of April
3, 1926, on "Syndicates and Collective Relations
of Labour." This law specifies clearly that syndicates, being an integral part of the nation's life, must
obtain the legal recognition of the State if they
expect to continue in existence. Furthermore, this
same law provides for the institution of the Labor
court, an instrument for the settlement of disputes arising from the interpretations of contracts,
regulations of labor, etc., which has proved to be
of the greatest usefulness in ameliorating the relationship of Capital and Labor. Finally, by declaring

in article No. 18: "The lock-out and the strike are forbidden in the Fascist State," this law eliminates with one stroke the greatest evil of modern economy; viz., the loss of production through voluntary or compulsory withdrawal of the worker from his work.

The next step is constituted by the Royal Decree of July 1, 1926, on "Functions of the Syndicates and Collective Relations of Labour."

This law, by specifying who may join the syndicates, by establishing the rules regulating the legal recognition—as well as the organization and the administration of syndical associations—by distinguishing various grades of syndical associations and by providing, with the institution of the corporations, liaison organs between associations of workers and employers, constitutes the keystone of the syndicalist organization of the Fascist State.

This syndicalist organization, generally thought of as a highly complicated structure, is in fact very simple. Employers and workers are grouped separately in professional and trade associations of first grade: local syndicates. These local syndicates are grouped in turn in higher grade syndical associations called Federations, each representing a single category or class of persons engaged in the same occupation.

These Federations, of a national character and therefore called National Federations, are also linked together whenever they cover activities having some ground in common. This link is provided by a syndical association of a still higher grade called Confederation, which joins all the National Federations of Syndicates engaged in one of the four branches of activity: Banking, Industry, Commerce and Agriculture.

There are thus eight general confederations: four of employers and four of employees engaged in the four main branches of national activity, and in addition, a ninth national confederation of intellectual workers constituted by the association of all persons engaged in the arts and professions, where no distinction is made between employer and worker.

The confederations are organs of a semi-political nature, because they are empowered to represent the interests of their affiliated syndicates in all their relationships with the national government and are empowered by the State to supervise, control and co-ordinate, on behalf of the government, the activities of the local syndicates in the provinces.

The duties of the local syndicates are:

(a) stipulate collective labor contracts for the workers in the territory of its jurisdiction;

(b) settle labor disputes;

(c) organize social welfare services and professional training courses for its members;

(d) appoint representatives to sit at boards or committees where the entire category should be represented.

The duties of the National Federations are:

(a) protect the interests of all categories represented and favour their economic and technical development;

(b) examine and settle economic and social questions concerning each of the categories represented;

(c) stipulate collective labor contracts between categories;

(d) regulate economic relations between them;

(e) supervise social welfare work and the technical and mental training of members;

(f) promote the development and improvement of production;

(g) appoint representatives of the various categories to sit at corporations and other councils where such categories should be represented.

Confederations have duties and functions very similar to those assigned to the National Federations, but they cover a wider and deeper range of action, inasmuch as they are concerned with the general interests of all National Federations represented by them. They represent thus the most important part of the entire edifice of Fascist Syndicalism.

Having constituted, on the basis of the workers' syndicates of socialistic origin, these nine national confederations, the Fascist reform has not only recognized the syndical movement, but has also legalized it, bringing it within the fold and under the aegis of the State.

Furthermore, in giving these syndicates laws and norms by which they must abide, Fascism has set for them the limits within which their activity can be explicated; has stated the amount of freedom allowed them, that amount only which is compatible with the freedom of other organizations and groups within the State, and has, finally, imposed upon them duties as well as rights: duties toward individuals, organizations, or the State itself, duties which they had ignored or never recognized before.

This entirely new economic and juridical conception of the social order received its first synthetic expression in the Labor Charter promulgated by the Grand Council of Fascism on April 21, 1927.

The importance of this new Charter of human rights and duties oversteps the national boundaries of the Italian State and the limits of time of the Fascist Revolution, to project itself across the whole western world and through the centuries yet to come.

By establishing as fundamental principles of individual and social life that: "Work in all its forms is a social duty;" that, "A Nation is an organism having ends, life, and means superior to the single individuals or groups of individuals composing it," and that, "A Nation is a moral entity," not an aggregate of individual elements, the Labor Charter advances a rightful claim to immortality.

In the Labor Charter we find for the first time that the activities of the syndical organizations, which are, more specifically, of an economic order for the federation and of an administrative and political order for the confederations, are still further enlarged in scope through the organization of the corporations.

Article VI of the Labor Charter states in effect that: "Corporations constitute the unitary organization of all the forces of production and integrally represent their interests. In virtue of this integral representation, since the interests of production are the interests of the nation, the corporations are recognized by the law as State organs. And representing the unitary interests of production, corporations may enforce binding regulations for the discipline of labor relations, as well as for the co-ordination of production whenever they are em-powered to do so by the affiliated associations."

It is thus current practice of the Fascist system that whenever disputes arise within a syndical or-ganization, they are referred to the respective cor-porations and, if necessary, to the Ministry of Corporations for an effort at conciliation. Should the conciliation fail, the dispute is brought before the Labor Court, which is nothing more than an ordinary Court of Appeal assisted by experts in the subject under dispute.

With the Labor Charter, therefore, we find for the first time that Corporations have assumed the meaning which specifically characterizes them to-day.

The very first definition of Corporations discloses in effect that they were originally conceived as pri-vate organs of collaboration between the various categories engaged in a determinate activity of pro-duction. (The term category is used here to repre-sent all the persons engaged in a given occupation, whether they be regular members of the syndicate or not.)

That first definition, embodied in Article 3 of the Law of April 3, 1926, reads as follows:

"Associations of employers and workers can be brought together by means of central liaison organs (future corporations) having high officials com-mon to both associations."

It was only Article 42 of the Royal Decree of July 1, 1926, which gave a national character to these "Liaison organs;" to use of the term corporation for the first time as their designation and to give finally, a concrete definition of the juridical aspects of corporations. This article and the three succeeding ones are here reported in full because of the great interest they present to students of political and economic sciences.

Article 42. "The liaison organs provided for by Article 3 of the Act of April 3, 1926, are of a national character. They bring together the national syndical organizations of the several factors of production: employers, intellectual and manual workers connected with a given branch of production, or with one or more given classes of enterprise. Organizations thus linked up form a corporation. The corporation is established by decree of the Minister of Corporations."

Article 43. "The corporation is not endowed with civil personality, but is an organ of State Administration. The decree whereby it it constituted shall specify its organization and regulate the duties of its central and local offices."

Article 44. "With a view to the achievement of these purposes, corporative organs are endowed with powers:

(a) to conciliate disputes that may arise between the affiliated organizations, and to issue rules as provided for in Article 10 of the Act of April 3, 1926;

(b) to promote, encourage and subsidize all initiatives aiming at the co-ordination and improvement of production;

(c) to set up labor exchanges wherever the need for them has arisen. Wherever such exchanges are established, independent mediation and the carrying out of other offices of the kind may be prohibited by Royal Decree, the special laws and regulations dealing with such matters always remaining in force;

(d) to regulate apprenticeship by issuing general compulsory rules on the matter and to supervize the observation thereof. Such rules are subject to all provisions made in collective labor contracts.

Article 45. "Presidents of corporative organs are appointed and removed by decree of the Minister of Corporations. Each corporation has a council composed of the delegates of the organizations affiliated thereto. On these councils the representation of the employers' organizations must be equal to that of the intellectual and manual workers taken together.

Following these preparatory provisions we find an Act of March 20, 1930, on the constitution of the "National Council of Corporations," which outlines the first organic constitution of Corporations; the "Resolution" of Nov. 13, 1933, of the Assembly of the National Council of Corporations drafted by Mussolini himself, upon the final definition and attributions of Corporations; and, finally, the Act of Feb. 5, 1934, on "The Formation and Functions of Corporations."

In their final definition Corporations are: "the organs which, under the aegis of the State, carry out the integral, organic and unitarian regulation of production with a view to the expansion of the wealth, political power and well-being of the Italian people." They represent, again in official words, "bridges thrown across the vertical lines of workers' syndicates and employers' federations," or, in other words, organs which allow workers and employers to come in contact and establish the co-operation necessary to replace that sterile class struggle which is the foundation of the obsolete Marxist philosophy of life. Following a geometrical pattern, the corporations would then represent the horizontal organizations, and the confederations the vertical organizations of the corporative system; the whole system being erected on a strictly syndical basis.

At present there are twenty-two corporations in existence, composed of delegates from employers and employees in all national activities, together with ex-officio members and technical experts.

The activities of the twenty-two corporations are co-ordinated through the National Council of Corporations and subject to the supreme authority of the Ministry of Corporations.

The twenty-two corporations are:

Eight Corporations for cycles of production embracing agriculture, industry and commerce: 1. Corporation of Cereals. 2. Corporation of Fruit, Vegetables and Flowers. 3. Corporation of Viticulture and Wine. 4. Corporation of Sugar-beet and Sugar. 5. Corporation of Edible Oil. 6. Corporation of Live-stock and Fisheries. 7. Corporation of Forestry, Lumber and Wood. 8. Corporation of Textiles.

Eight Corporations for cycles of production embracing industry and commerce: 9. Corporation of Metal and Engineering. 10. Corporation of Chemical Trades. 11. Corporation of Clothing Trades. 12. Corporation of Printing, Publishing and Paper. 13. Corporation of Building Trades and Housing. 14. Corporation of Water, Gas and Electricity. 15.

Corporation of Mining and Quarrying. 16. Corporation of Glass-ware and Pottery.

Six Corporations covering occupations productive of services: 17. Corporation of the Arts and Professions, comprising four sections: legal professions; medical profession; technical professions; the arts. 18. Corporation of Inland Transports, comprising four sections: railways, tramways and inland navigation; transports by motor; traffic auxiliaries; communications by telephone, radio-telephony. 19. Corporation of Sea and Air Transports. 20. Corporation of Hotel Industry. 21. Corporation of Credit and Insurance, comprising three sections: banks, savings banks and public institutions; insurance. 22. Corporation of Entertainments.

With the classification of the twenty-two corporations the description of the syndical organization of the Fascist State is finally complete.

Looked at in its totality this organization appears as an hierarchical arrangement which proceeds from the local syndicates, through the National Federations, the nine general Confederations, the twenty-two Corporations, the National Council of Corporations, and the Ministry of Corporations, in a continuously ascending series of attributes, duties and powers, and in a continuously widening sphere of tasks and influence, duplicating in the economic order the greater social hierarchical arrangement of the Fascist Nation and the Fascist State as a whole.

PART THREE

FASCISM AS A HISTORICAL PROCESS

CHAPTER XII

THE HISTORICAL BACKGROUND
OF FASCISM

Fascism, to be rightly understood, must be placed in relief against its own historical background. It is this background which alone can give depth, and with the depth, significance and expression to otherwise apparently shallow and meaningless characteristics and unintelligible, intricate aspects.

Why did Fascism have its birth in Italy and not elsewhere; why was the man Benito Mussolini chosen by destiny to give concrete shape to the new social and economic gospel; why did the reaction to Individualism as a way of life, begin only with the advent of Fascism and not before: these are questions which must be answered and can be answered only by a reconstruction of what forms the historical background of Fascism.

Three main spiritual forces have shaped the soul of the culture of the western world: the Renaissance, the Reformation, the Revolution.

The Renaissance, releasing all the pent-up energy

accumulated within the inner depths of Being through a long succession of unarticulated centuries, gave birth to the individual's consciousness of his individuality. The Reformation, testing and proving the right of the individual's freedom of belief, brought about the independence of the individual's spiritual life from the constraint of the Church.

The Revolution, proclaiming and asserting that Liberty is not the privilege of a few men, but the inalienable right of every man, brought about the realization of those conditions which made possible the final triumph of Individualism and the initial decay of all human Institutions.

The measure in which these three main forces acted upon the life of a country, in that measure did the life of that country become representative expression of the soul of Western culture.

Italy, which experienced the full impact of the Renaissance, but was left out of the main stream of the Reformation, and only indirectly felt the consequences of the Revolution, cannot be said, therefore, to be as representative of this culture as other nations which experienced to their fullest extent the action of all the three forces mentioned above.

The historian who attempts thus to trace the fundamental cause for the Italian birth of Fascism cannot fail to attribute it primarily to this difference of causes and effects; of action of outside spiritual forces and reaction of the inner essence of a nation.

Nowhere else is that organic necessity of Destiny, which Oswald Spengler saw conditioning the very aspects of the world-as-history, so evident as in this correspondence existing between the soul of western culture and the expression of life of a western nation.

But this evidence becomes well-nigh inoppugnable, when from the general consideration of the three determining forces, we pass to the particular consideration of the instruments created by these forces in the final period of realization of their action.

These instruments can be briefly stated to be:

Intellectual means: A philosophy which, under the various names of Materialism, Naturalism, Realism, etc., furnished man with a mechanistic view of the world and his life, a view which had no place for such intangible things as God, the Soul, and the Ideals.

Social means: A Liberal doctrine which predicated upon the idea of Liberty as a means of providing a fuller life to all the people, made of this Liberty the privilege of a small class only.

Political means: The institution of Parliamentary Democracy, which, founded on the belief that the realization of Democracy in Politics is compatible with social and economic inequality, lost all foundation when this belief was thoroughly disproved by the actual course of human events.

Economic means: The institution of Capitalism which born out of the exploitation of the working class, became in the end the most effective means of domination and power of the Capitalist class.

In the ultimate analysis the triumph of Individualism as a philosophy and a way of life rests upon the adequacy of these means to fulfill the purpose for which they were devised.

Now it is a historical truism that these means

which have proved only partially adequate in England, France, or the United States of America, have instead shown themselves utterly inadequate in Italy.

We know of course that owing to differences of traditions, of habits, of laws, life is bound to assume different aspects in different parts of the western world; but that does not explain the fundamental inadequacy of those instruments of intellectual, social, political and economic life which have otherwise brought about the complete triumph of Individualism elsewhere.

Something radically important, something which has to do with the very core of being of a nation, must constitute the essential difference. It is in the research of this unknown something the main purpose of this investigation of the historical background of Fascism, and, although the research cannot be but a summary one within the limits of space of this chapter, and the investigation cannot consequently be complete, the purpose is too enticing not to be fulfilled, even if it is to be fulfilled only in a partial and very ineffective way.

To begin with, no philosophical doctrine could be more utterly alien to the very spirit of Italy than Materialism, or any of its equivalent: Positivism, Naturalism, Pragmatism, etc.

Benedetto Croce expresses the sentiment of all Italians when he says: "The new vision saw no longer the true and the whole man, in whom the struggle between spirit and body must be fought out, but man reduced to the level of an animal, always and only body and flesh, in spite of certain semblances and false appearances of generous impulses and lofty yearnings, which, if scrutinized, revealed themselves as nervous disturbances or frankly as the results of neurasthenia. Far out of sight was placed not the real mystery, the sacred mystery, which contains within it all these values whose secret it does not reveal, but our lack of knowledge, our more or less provisional ignorance, with the assumption that perhaps one day some combination of atoms or the like would be found which would explain everything and enable us to produce in the laboratory life with all its products commonly called spiritual."

To this doctrine which is the negation of the true life and the true mission of man, the Italian race opposes its deep, unfathomable sense of the existence of those great, everlasting realities called God, Fatherland, Soul and Ideals; its mystic intuition that belief in God, in the Soul, the Fatherland and the power of Ideals is the greatest molding force of human life; its mysterious, instinctive knowledge of the truth that life is more than raiment, and that only in the fulfillment of its duties through the redeeming and ennobling spiritual process of sacrifice and sorrow, can life have any meaning and acquire any worth.

If a materialistic philosophy is therefore a necessary basis for the triumph of Individualism — and that such is the case nobody can deny it — that triumph could never be complete in Italy, or, if brought to conclusion, could never be everlasting.

The philosophy of Italy has been consistently an Idealistic philosophy all through those centuries characterized by the rise and the affirmation of Individualism. One lonely soul: Roberto Ardigó, made a tentative excursion in the barren field of Positivism, but his unfruitful excursion could furnish no sound philosophical basis for the erection of a stable edifice of individualistic aims.

It is highly symptomatic, therefore, the fact that the Fascist anti-materialistic reaction was chronologically preceded by the enunciation of Benedetto Croce's philosophy of Historical Idealism and Giovanni Gentile's philosophy of Actual Idealism. Different as these two aspects of Idealism may be, they still have one thing in common: viz., the characteristic of being the antithesis of any doctrine which glorifies the individual as lord and center of the whole universe, and the individual's materialistic aims as the very aims of this universe.

When we pass next from a consideration of the philosophical doctrine underlying the whole practice of Individualism, to the consideration of the Liberal Theory of laissez-faire, which underlies all relationship of the Individual and the State and of the Individual and the People in modern western states, we notice even more forcefully than before how deficient the full realization of this doctrine could ever be within the life of the Italian Nation.

Why the liberal doctrine of maximum possible freedom for the individual could be of successful practical application it is necessary that two important elements of individual and social life be verified: first, the average man should be so desirous of enjoying this maximum amount of freedom as to be willing to sacrifice for its realization all other ideals, all other purposes; second, the nexus of economic, political and social relations should be such as to allow the possibility for the full explication of such freedom.

Of these two conditions, the second has never been realized in any country at any time of human history, the first has never been realized in Italy.

This sweeping statement of the average Italian man's limited enthusiasm for freedom must, of course, be substantiated and should be substantiated with a thorough analysis of the formation of the Italian character. It will suffice here to point out that the peculiar experience of life of the Anglo-Saxon race which led the Anglo-Saxon man to taste the forbidden fruit of freedom and to make of it an idol to worship, has not, and could not have been duplicated in the life of the Italian race. The Italian man has always held that respect for authority has precedence over any desire for liberty.

The words of Mazzini on this question are definitive and worthy of reproduction in extent: "On every side the doubt has arisen—of what advantage is liberty? Of what advantage equality, which is in fact but the liberty of all? What is the free man but an activity, a force, to be put in motion? In what direction shall he move? As chance or caprice may direct? But that is not life, it is a mere succession of acts, of phenomena, of emissions of vitality without bond, relation, or continuity; it is anarchy. The liberty of the one will inevitably clash with the liberty of others; constant strife will arise between individual and individual with consequent loss of force and waste of the productive faculties vouchsafed to us, faculties which we are bound to regard as sacred. The liberty of all, if ungoverned by any general directing law, will but lead to a state of warfare among men, a warfare rendered all the more cruel and inexorable by the virtual equality of the antagonists."

The expressed thought of Mazzini, which is the unexpressed thought of every Italian, demonstrates that the Liberal doctrine, entirely alien to the Italian spirit, grafted upon the body of Italian life, but never become an integral part of Italian life, could not fail to be discarded whenever the needs of the times demanded it and the favorable occasion arose.

When, from this general survey of Liberalism, we pass to consideration of the specific application of its principles to the field of Politics, we notice that such application, which has found its truest embodiment in that form of representative government called Parliamentary Democracy, is least adapted to continue the traditions of Italian political life.

Parliamentary Democracy means a legislative body, which constitutes the supreme power of the State, and an executive body responsible to the legislature; the whole system resting upon the basis of the election of selected individuals to represent the general interests of the people.

The successful working of this system requires that a long practice of self-government has made the people capable of being independent from high authorities without lapsing into anarchy and an equally long practice of the elective process has made of them masters of the difficult art of rightly choosing their best representatives.

Both types of practices have been foreign to the political life of the Italian nation up to the time of the "Risorgimento," and whatever experience of them has been accrued since that fateful year of 1848, which saw the first Italian Constitution follow in the wake of the European liberal movement, this experience of less than a century of time can hardly be called sufficient to make of the Italian people masters of the art of representative government and enthusiastic followers of democratic forms.

Finally, when we remember that the whole history of the Italian culture is not a history of mass expression and mass achievement but the history of the personal, highly individualized, and highly characteristic contribution of each single Italian to the cumulative effort required by the creation of such a culture, we can look with but dismay to the imposition of Capitalism upon the economic life of the Italian people.

The success of Capitalism is based upon the subjection of a whole class of people to a standardization of personal work; the subjection of the whole nation to a standardization of national taste; the subjection of each national State itself to a common international standard of life.

Capitalism, in other words, apart from all the other numerous evils entrained in its wake, as experienced by all western nations alike, represents for Italy the antithesis and the nemesis of that aspect of her true national spirit, reflected in the economic life of her people.

The history of modern Italy is thus the actual, luminous proof that Capitalism, like Parliamentary Democracy, like the laissez-faire doctrine, like all the other means developed by triumphant Individualism to render its triumph more complete, more lasting in the modern western world, was to prove utterly inadequate to bring about such a triumph in Italy, and, what is a true blessing, was to be the determining factor of the beginning of that reaction to Individualism which was to be called Fascism.

The history of modern Italy begins with the year 1870. The selection of this date may seem somewhat arbitrary, and yet it is conditioned by the very course of national political development of the country.

If ten historians were asked to name the dates of the two most important events in the history of Italy from the standpoint of national political development, there is no doubt that nine of them would not fail to suggest for such dates the year 456 which saw the curtain fall definitely upon the last act of the Roman Empire and the year 1870 which saw Rome become capital again of a re-born Italy.

An interval of approximatively fourteen centuries divides thus the disappearance of the Italian (Roman) State from its re-appearance under a truly national flag and with a truly national character.

During these fourteen centuries a succession of events such as the rapid spread of an appalling shadow over the civilized zones of the western world, the growth of the temporal power of the Popes, the revival of learning, the Renaissance symphony, the Reformation dirge, the discovery of America, the invention of printing, the discovery of gun-powder, the birth of the National States, the triumph of the principle of representative government, the French upheaval, the Napoleonic tragedy, the Industrial revolution; events which had actually transformed the face of the earth, had made of Italy, in particular, a land of many social and political organizations with different, and often conflicting aims, interests, laws, traditions and customs. No country was thus more unprepared than Italy was in the year 1870, to support the life of a modern national state with a political structure founded upon the principle of representative government, a social structure founded on liberal principles, an economic structure founded on capitalistic principles, and a producing organization founded on industry and the machine.

And, yet, if Italy had to have her place in the sun, if Italy had to conquer anew her primacy among the nations of the earth, if Italy was to lead again the western world in the race of progress, Italy had to adapt herself in the shortest possible time to the ways of the western world.

Such was the thought of those who directed the course of Italian life in those fateful years which began with the entrance of the troops of King Victor Emmanuel the Second into Papal Rome and ended with the entrance of Fascist troops into the Rome of King Victor Emmanuel the Third.

A new course of national life requires always a new set of Ideals as moving force and final goal of this life.

The ideals which had inspired the course of Italian life through the crucial years of the "Risorgimento" and up to the year 1870, were the Mazzinian Ideals; that is: Moral and Religious education as basis of all education, Devotion to God, the Fatherland and the Family as basis of all social life, Duty, Sacrifice and Respect for Authority as basis of all individual life.

These ideals had inspired all the great patriots; these ideals can be said, therefore, to have brought about the Italian "Risorgimento," and the re-birth of Italy as a national state. (We must always re-member that the "Risorgimento" was the master-piece of a score of great spirits, seconded by a few thousand followers, and not the work of the masses).

But beginning with the year 1870, a conviction became more and more generalized: the conviction that these Ideals had seen their best days and that their practice could not suffice to cope with the realities of everyday life as it was being shaped by the new forces at work in its midst.

The year 1876 saw the triumph of this view with the fall of the last cabinet of the "Right," composed of members of the "Old Guard," heirs of the tradition of Mazzini, Gioberti, Cavour and Garibaldi, and the coming into power of the first cabinet of the "Left" composed of representatives of the new social and economic classes forming within the nation.

If the new cabinet knew very well which ideals were to be forsaken, it certainly did not know equally well which ideals had to take their place. There was abroad a vague feeling that a more demo-cratic policy should be the policy of the new gov-ernment, and this feeling the men of the "Left" attempted to crystallize in a series of reforms which began, naturally enough, with the extension of the franchise.

Of all the attractions that a government which

attempts to win the favor of the people, can offer to the people, the extension of the franchise is surely the easiest to grant and the surest to bring result.

We find thus that beginning with 1882 when the first extension was granted and ending with 1913, when Giovanni Giolitti increased finally the number of electors from three millions to seven millions at one time, the demagogic governments of Italy, succeeded in power from 1876 to 1913, did exactly what all demagogic governments do all over the world: offered as bait to the pariah of society the magic, and yet meaningless, privilege of a vote to persons whom he cannot know and for issues which he cannot understand.

The supreme fault of the Liberal democratic doctrine, is that of positing the realization of the abstract principle of the individual right to vote as the *ideal* to be realized, without placing such realization in relation to other features of the individual's life, such as his moral and intellectual fitness and his relationship to the social and economic environment.

Little did the men in power care whether those to whom they gave the right to vote were prepared, spiritually and materially, to exercise this right. Little did they care that an enormous amount of preparatory work had to be done to make the people of Italy—molded by fourteen centuries of campanilistic rivalry into warring champions of particular interests—conscious of the supreme interest of the nation as a whole.

Little did they care that a long process of formal and symbolic education was necessary to make of

185

the southern farmer—degraded by centuries of a most abject life lived under that blood-exacting foreign domination called by Gladstone "true negation of God"—a worthy citizen of a modern state.

The process of extension of the franchise went merrily on and corruption, bribery, falsehood, and crime accompanied the triumph in Italy of the hallowed principle of representative government.

But representative government means not only the electorate, it means also the parliament. Parliament means in turn party system, and party system, contrasting sets of ideologies as basis of all political life.

Up to 1870, when the only parties of the Italian parliament were those which existed in the parliament of the small Kingdom of Piedmont, the interests of the masses were the concern of all representatives. But after 1870 the masses began to feel that their best interests would be protected by the election of men whose ideologies were born out of impact with the realities of their every-day life. And because these realities were of a very materialistic nature, those ideologies were of a very prosaic sort.

The standard of Italian political life began thus to fall lower and lower with each succeeding year after 1870, culminating with the triumph of men who renegaded and despised the very Ideals which had brought about the re-birth of Italy. Vainly did men like Giosue' Carducci or like Alfredo Oriani protest against the existing order of things, auspicating the return to old grandeur and classic ideals. The poet sang to people who could appreciate only the sensual charm of beautiful words and melodic rhymes, and the prophet spoke to multitudes who could not understand him and did not want to understand him.

In the meantime, the parliament had become the arena for the final issues of the war of classes, lifted from the market-place into the aeropagus, and fought over by a score or more of parties, differing only in names from each other, because all were concerned with one thing and one thing only—how to be able to appropriate the biggest part of the spoils of the State.

The supreme good, the supreme interests of the State were the concern of nobody in particular and utterly forgotten and forsaken in the mad scramble for power, for advantages, for wealth.

Upon such parody of a true liberal-democratic political practice, the foundations were laid for the transformation of Italy from an eminently agricultural country with a residual feudal form of economy, to an industrial land with a modern capitalist form of economy.

Lacking, as Italy does, all raw materials essential for a successful industrial life, this transformation required a vision of the problems to be solved which the leaders could not supply.

The liberal leaders thought that it was enough to let the State interfere the least possible with men and events; that everything would aright itself in the end.

The working class leaders had just discovered Karl Marx and "The Capital" and were preaching a materialistic interpretation of history and the war of classes as new gospel of social destruction if not social salvation.

In the meantime, while industries multiplied, the number of industrial establishments which amounted in 1870 to less than five thousand increased nearly one hundred-fold by 1914 and Capitalism flourished—the capital invested in limited liability companies which amounted to only two hundred million dollars in 1870 increased to two billions by 1914—the State became a thing to abuse and ridicule, the nation was precipitated into a condition of anarchy, the standard of living continued falling always lower and lower and the working class, for all the preaching of Socialism, or perhaps as a consequence of it, was drifting openly into the communist fold.

But, strange as it may seem, the world war was the thing that indirectly brought about the salvation of Italy; indirectly, because it must never be thought of as the prime mover of the forces which brought about the birth of Fascism.

Once more, as always happens, it was a subjective reaction to an objective thing: the impact of the war experience upon the consciousness of a sensitive man, and the fortunate coincidence that this man had a soul great enough to encompass the true meaning of this most tragic of all tragic events, that caused the birth of that new way of life called Fascism.

The World war, the Italian nation and her history, the man Benito Mussolini with his past and his war experience, constitute, at the same time, the indissoluble triad responsible for the *Italian* birth of Fascism.

At it is, the war reconciled for a time all opposing interests, all class struggles, all enemy forces, within each of the national boundaries, delaying but not halting the inevitable process of disintegration and decay of the western world.

It was only when the close of the war found no other element, no other agency, no other power but Fascism, which could halt the last stage of the conflict between the disintegrating forces of Individualism and the integrating forces of social laws, traditions and customs, that the change of the whole course of life of the Italian nation determined the beginning of that nation's reaction to the doctrine and the practice of Individualism.

But if it is true that the triad: World war—Italian nation—Benito Mussolini, brought about the birth of Fascism in the city of Milan on the twenty-third day of March, 1919, it is nevertheless also true that obscure forces originated within the very heart of western civilization more than four centuries ago and, acquiring always greater intensity with the passing of time, were sooner or later to bring about a revolution in the way of life of the western world.

The world war, which has been erroneously made the actual prime mover of the forces which brought about the birth of Fascism, was a symptom, not a cause of the process of decay of western culture.

And because the world war is still a fact of contemporaneous chronicle rather than an event of past history, its description; the description of its causes, its features and its effects, has no place in an exposition of the historical background of Fascism.

This exposition ends, therefore, with the hope-

189

ful note of a man who has found himself in Fascism, and of a nation which has found in Fascism its salvation.

CHAPTER XIII

TWO FORERUNNERS OF FASCISM

GIANBATTISTA VICO

Fascism is a creature of the twentieth century, but this century, in turn, is the child of former ages: a product of those other centuries which have preceded it in the realm of time.

The invisible and imponderable forces which moulded the aspects assumed by this most characteristic phenomenon of modern times are indeed manifestations of the very thoughts left in heritage by the representative thinkers of the past.

Thus it can be affirmed that the reaction to Individualism, whose final triumph is now called Fascism, began, not in the year 1919, but in the year 1620 when Gianbattista Vico published his first draft of the "New Science," setting himself resolutely against the individualistic philosophy of life of the Renaissance and the dissolving spirit of his times.

It has been rightly said, ". . . the philosophy of

his age tended to dissolve society, to dissociate men, to lose sight of humanity, nations and families in the contemplation of isolated individuals. . . ." The philosophy of Vico, instead, was "a philosophy which would give an account of men not as solitary, but as social beings; which would promote social union, strength and progress." It is with Vico, then, that we must begin our study of the two greatest forerunners of Fascism.

There are, in the history of mankind, singular names of men who were destined to exercise a powerful influence upon the intellectual life of their nation, but have remained, nevertheless, practically unknown to the rest of the world.

One of those names is that of Gianbattista Vico.

Whatever claims Italy may advance in those most magnificent realms of thought called philosophy of history, philosophy of language, and philosophy of law and morals, it remains an undisputed fact that those claims are based upon the works of Vico and, principally, upon his masterpiece "La Scienza Nuova" (The New Science).

"The New Science," says Giovanni Gentile, "is the profound intuition of this great truth: that man, the true man who sings of his sorrows and his hopes; who thinks and explains his thought; who founds religion and with religion the city, the law and the State; and wages war; and passes from barbarism to civilization, is not a particular individual, neither a sum of individuals, but only and always Man."

"The New Science" is, in other words, a tribute to that hidden and yet so manifestly apparent unity which underlies the multiform activity of man.

In the historical process, this unity reveals itself with an identity of the substance of those external forms of social organization through which man expresses his social life with each succeeding civilization. According to Vico, a law of cycles of "Corsi e Ricorsi" is at work throughout the course of human history.

This law of cycles renders all hopes of a continuous, lineal, unbroken universal progress, baseless and senseless. Each civilization is a spiritual entity complete unto itself and, at no time of human history does a certain form of civilization constitute a progress or a regress upon another and different one. And the very elements which determine the character of a civilization are not evolved in succession of time, but are co-existent from the day of its birth.

For Vico the entire history of mankind is but the eternal Idea of that history as it exists in the Divine Mind, realized and manifested in actual events. The true philosophy of history seemed to him to lie beneath and beyond all appearances in the Divine Ideal.

The philosophy of history, conceived thus as the revelation of the activity of the Spirit immanent in the life of man and, at all times, equal to itself, imparts a new dignity to the life of today because the need has disappeared to justify it as a preparation for a better life of the morrow.

It is the life of today which, according to Vico, must be brought back to the vision of the Ideals which ought to govern the World of Man, not the life of a hypothetical tomorrow which may never dawn.

If then, we accept the "New Science" as the truest interpretation of the phenomena characterizing the unfolding of human history, we must accept also the consequence of the necessity of renewing the spiritual springs of life whenever they have run dry, and there is danger of a new return to barbarism, a new "Decline of the West."

Not only has Fascism accepted this logical consequence, but has made it its cardinal reason of being, fully convinced of the truth that Vico has seen very deep and very far into that occult realm where the Parcae spin incessantly the web of man's destiny. And as in any cycle of world history, the beginnings of the cycle are characterized by the stress placed on the heroic qualities inherent in the human soul—qualities which are in periods of decadence thoroughly displaced by the lower instincts of our animal nature—Fascism opens the new cycle with the affirmation that "the life of the Fascist feeds on heroism and has sacrifice as its goal."

These beautiful words testify of the profound idealism underlying the whole philosophy of Fascism, and, if in reading them, the question is asked whether Fascism is not too idealistic, even visionary, perhaps the question may be answered recalling the words of Joseph Chamberlain: "Let no one fancy that anything great can be achieved in this world without a purely ideal power being at work."

Having discovered its cardinal reason for existence in the need of a renewal of the spiritual springs of life, in the need of bringing to a close this period of spiritual decadence and of opening a new cycle of world history vivified by heroism and marked by sacrifice, Fascism finds in Vico other directing elements of its philosophy of life, elements which contrast deeply with those current in our present mode of living.

A great wrong has been done by Science to mankind; that of having required the almost complete devotion of the intellectual energies of man throughout three whole centuries.

We have been able thus to achieve a partial mastery of the external world, minimizing in the meantime the importance of our internal world.

It is high time now—Fascism says—that we should turn from the world without to the world within and try to achieve, if not a complete mastery of it, at least some understanding of it for our own salvation. But the approach to the kingdom within must proceed along a different path than the path of Science.

By following the scientific process of knowledge we comprehend the world of nature by decomposing it in parts, analyzing these parts separately and then trying to achieve a synthesis out of our partial analysis.

We all believe that this process of the mind approaching the world of nature from without is the only one truly apt to reach the core of being. But Vico, in his "New Science," shows how utterly childish is the naive belief that science can ever furnish us with the ultimate truth. His words, on this subject, are truly worth reporting:

"Truth is simply Fact; that is, what is Made. In God there is the first truth, because He is the first maker; infinite truth, because He is the maker of all things; absolutely accurate truth, because He has present to Himself all the elements, both external and internal of things, seeing that He contains them. But the human mind, because it is limited, and because to all things external to and apart from itself, can reach only their outward conditions; it cannot comprehend them."

Also: "God knows all things because He contains in himself the elements of which He composes all things; but man, in endeavoring to know things, must recourse to dividing them. Therefore, human science is a kind of anatomy of nature."

And: "Seeing that human science is born of a defect of the mind—namely, of its extreme littleness—in consequence of which it is external to all things, contains nothing of what it desires to know and so cannot produce the truth which it seeks to ascertain; those sciences are the most certain which expiate the defect in which they originate and which resemble divine science by the creative activity they involve."

No more effective blow could ever be dealt to that naive assumption of modern man, that in science he has fashioned for himself an instrument of thought and research which will necessarily bring him to the discovery of truth, than the blow dealt by those words of Vico.

And that fallacy, commonly held, that all great discoveries are the product only of perseverance and patience, remains for Vico a pious hope, because he maintains that original discoveries can be made only by men imbued with "the vision and the faculty divine," who can see and comprehend things which remain unseen and unknown to the great mass of mankind.

It is necessary then to agree with Fascist thinkers

196

that the pursuit of knowledge about the true nature of things must needs follow two very distinct paths.

Through the first, the path of Science, we can gain an understanding of the laws which govern the world of matter, the world of time and space, the world of facts, of action, of movement; in a word, the world of Becoming:—through the other, the path of Philosophy, we can gain an insight into the world of Being, the world of Ideas, the world of Values, which is not in time nor in space; the world which exists in the Divine Mind and to which belongs the true nature of Man.

Rightly, Mussolini, speaking at the Congress of Sciences in Bologna the thirty-first day of October, 1926, said, "There is a zone which is reserved less to research than to the meditation of the supreme aims of life. Consequently, science starts from the data of experience but ends fatally in philosophy; and, only philosophy can illuminate the path of science and bring it to the vision of the Universal Idea."

Such a task as that which Fascism has undertaken, of educating the new generation to a revaluation of Science and the search—through a rebirth of philosophical studies—of a new approach to the life of the spirit, the problems of conscience and the world of the soul, is part of the legacy of Vico.

But this legacy is not exhausted as yet. There is, in fact, a realm of human relationships, where the realization of the fundamental Ideal of human life —Justice, ought to reign supreme. In this realm, the realm of Law, Vico threw the inquisitive beam

197

of light of his searching mind. What he saw is that laws are not a thing apart from the motives which originated them or the outward conditions in which they had their birth.

Law has its birth because man is a social animal. Law has its reason for being because it harmonizes the wants of the individual with the requirements of the social organism.

Furthermore, while law must concern itself with the regulation of social relationships, it should not concern itself with external punishments. The greatest punishment that the guilty individual can ever be subjected to is the feeling of having violated the inner law of his conscience, and no man ever sinned against the light within.

"Because the edge of conscience becomes blunted," says W. Knight, reporting Vico's thought, "and the pain it inflicts ceases to be sharp enough, the interests of society are compromised in such a manner that external and material pain must be added by human law to the purely internal and spiritual pain which follows wrong-doing. The external law and punishment, must, however, be modeled on the internal law and punishment. The voice of the judge without should correspond to what would be the voice of the judge within, were it allowed to be clearly heard. Otherwise penal law becomes the expression of arbitrariness and vengeance."

Ideas as revolutionary as those of Vico could not remain forever without having practical actuation in some form of social organization. Fascism maintains, therefore, that the main task of that supreme being among all social agencies: the State, is not the task of building always bigger and better jails but the task of making always a little brighter the light within, of raising the general level of conscience of the people, of bringing the people to understand and to acknowledge the nobler claims of the moral life, and lead them, thus, by a continuous, progressive, constant process of education, to the vision of the higher things of life, the only things that truly matter and are worth living for.

From what has been said so far it is possible to visualize already the enormous influence of Vico's philosophy on Fascist thought. But this influence extends still farther, reaches still deeper recesses, puts still more tenacious roots within the inner core of Facism.

Knowing that the principle of Authority is one of the three cardinal principles, which, according to Fascism, must rule the conduct of life, it can be already stated that the main importance of Vico lies in his rigid conception of Authority as the ultimate criterion of the conduct of social life. The right to individual judgment in all matters which concern social relationships must be abdicated for the right of society as a whole; and this right must be vested in those who hold the supreme authority in the commonwealth or the State.

And if the question is raised regarding those to whom the supreme authority shall be delegated, Vico answers unhesitantly that such authority belongs by right to those who can claim a fuller, higher and more immediate relationship with the Divine.

Thus, nothing could be more foreign to the

thought of Vico and, consequently, to Fascist thought, than the assumption which is the basis of all modern theory of government; namely, the assumption that those who govern must derive their right by the common consent of the governed. For Vico, Authority, which he defines: "The source of eternal justice," must be independent from, and above the will of the people. Any state or any commonwealth in which the paramount issues are dependent upon the expression of such a will must needs end in confusion and anarchy.

The position which Vico takes on the question of Authority finds its counterpart in the position which he takes on the issue of Liberty. In one case, as in the other, he is against the trend of his time and of our modern times; against the dissolving power of Individualism clamoring for independence from all authority and freedom from all constraint.

For Vico, Liberty is something entirely different than what it is commonly held to be: the possibility of doing what one likes, of getting what one wishes, of acting as one pleases. For Vico, Liberty means that power, "which is proper of the human will of keeping within bounds the passions of the mind, as well as the instincts of the body, because with these acts of supremacy over one's own self is true Liberty born."

For Vico, Liberty takes, in other words, the same meaning which it has received in the Fascist reform: the meaning of supreme directive authority of the individual life of man, of the foundation of social life, of begetter of morality.

With Vico, Fascism is born and Individualism begins to die.

GIUSEPPE MAZZINI

The reaction to Individualism begun by Vico found its greatest exponent in Giuseppe Mazzini a century later.

The life of Mazzini is the most luminous example of the life of a man spent entirely at the service of an Idea.

Having one faith, one purpose, one ideal, this life develops from the beginning to the end as a musical composition that gradually unfolds itself from a single theme. And as a musical composition dies out when all possibilities of variation of the theme are exhausted, so the life of Mazzini comes to its end when the Idea is become a Reality, and it has fulfilled in this way its own destiny.

But Mazzini was not only a great Italian patriot, he was also and mainly an inward seer, a profound mystic and a highly imaginative prophet.

He was, in effect, the first of the moderns to become aware that Individualism as a way of life can lead mankind only to anarchy, to chaos and ruin. He was the first to realize that human history can offer patent examples of the truth that the triumph of Individualism brings about the debacle of Authority, of Order, of Law; the downfall, in short, of civilization itself.

Writing of the last days of the Roman Empire, he draws an ominous picture: "The sky was dark, the heavens void; the people strangely agitated, or motionless in stupor. Whole nations disappeared.

Others lifted their heads as if to view their fall. Throughout the world was a dull rumble of dissolution. All trembled; the heavens and the earth. Man was hideous to behold. Placed between two infinites, he had no consciousness of either; none of his future, nor of his past. All belief was extinct. Man had no faith in his gods, no belief in the republic. Society was no more. Great principles were no more. The Fatherland was no more. Material interests existed alone. The soul of man had fled: the senses reigned supreme. . . . Such were the times; they resembled our own," wrote Mazzini a century ago. How much more exactly and appropriately to *our* times, instead, could his words be applied!

The denial of Ideals, the loss of Religion, the debasement of Morality, the nullification of Authority, the disregard of Law, the worship of Wealth, the destruction of the Family; all are symptoms of a life which has moved away from its true human basis, and is reverting to a condition of purely animal existence.

The picture is dark but not hopeless. A ray of hope dawns on it as soon as we become conscious that the whole process of history can be altered and diverted to a fruitful end, if to the doctrine of the Rights of Man we substitute the doctrine of the Duties of Man, as moving force of the plans, the purposes and the actions of individual beings and social groups.

And it is no exaggeration to affirm that it is precisely on the enunciation of the Doctrine of the Duties of Man that the main glory of Mazzini rests, and his influence upon the whole western world is due.

When he states, "We must convince men that they must obey one only law, here on earth; that each one of them must live not for himself but for others; that the object of their life is not to be more or less happy, but to make themselves and others better; that to fight against injustice and error for the benefit of their brothers is not only a RIGHT but a DUTY; a duty not to be neglected without sin—the duty of their whole life." Mazzini sounds unknowingly the battle-cry of that philosophy of life which constitutes the true essence of Fascism.

The great irony of history, according to Mazzini, is the fact that the theory of Rights has deceived the very hopes and expectations of those who shed their blood and gave their lives for its triumph. "Of what use," he asks, "is the recognition of their rights to those who have no means of exercising them? What does liberty mean to those who have no means to profit by it? For all those constrained to battle with hunger is not liberty but an illusion and a bitter irony? If the idea of rights inherent in human nature is today so generally accepted, why, then, has the condition of the people not improved? Why is the consumption of products, instead of being divided equally among all the members of the social body, concentrated in the hands of a small number of men forming a new aristocracy? Why has the new impulse given to industry and commerce produced not the well-being of the many, but the luxury of the few?"

But the doctrine of Rights has not only deceived the people; it has also failed to provide the needed framework for a satisfactory human life.

"Certainly Rights do exist," says Mazzini, "but where the rights of an individual come into conflict with those of another, how can we hope to reconcile and harmonize them, without appealing to something superior to all rights? And where the rights of an individual, or of many individuals, clash with the rights of the Country, to what tribunal are we to appeal? If the right to well-being, to the greatest possible well-being, belongs to every living person, who will solve the difficulty between the working-man and the manufacturer? If the right to existence is the first and inviolable right of every man, who shall demand the sacrifice of that existence for the benefit of other men? Will you demand it in the name of Country, of Society, of the multitude of your brothers? What is Country, in the opinion of those of whom I speak, but the place in which our individual rights are most secure? What is Society but a collection of men who have agreed to bring the strength of the many in support of the rights of each? After having taught the individual that Society is established for the purpose of assuring him the exercise of his rights, would you ask him to sacrifice them all to Society, to submit himself if need be, to continuous toil, to prison, to exile, for the sake of improving it? After having preached to him everywhere that the object of life is well-being, would you all at once bid him give up well-being and life itself to free his country from the foreigner, or to procure better conditions for a class which is not his own? After having talked to him for years of material interests, how can you maintain that, finding wealth and power in his reach, he ought not to stretch out his hand to grasp them, even to the injury of his brothers? And even in a society constituted on a basis more just than our own, who shall convince a believer in the theory of rights that he must work for a common purpose and devote himself to the development of the social Idea?"

This series of questions propounded by Mazzini was never answered. Yet questions like these are of tragic import to mankind and must need be answered if social life is to be preserved in our times. It is thus that Fascism, making its own the central thought of Mazzini has found an answer in the substitution of the theory of the Duties of Man to the theory of the Rights of Man. By stressing our duty toward God and our Country, toward the Family and our fellow men, toward the State and our spiritual heritage, Fascism has furnished man with a new framework for the development of a meaningful individual life and a satisfactory social life.

In this way Fascism is the direct heir of Mazzini's thought. But the heritage of Mazzini is not exhausted by the doctrine of the Duties of Man. It was Mazzini, indeed, who clearly saw that although life requires a norm of conduct in the conception of Duty, a supreme law in the Moral law, there still remains an enigmatic query which needs be answered, namely: What constitutes the motive power of human history?

It was in the answer to such a query that the mystic genius of Mazzini found perhaps its greatest expression.

The essence of human history, he says, is the

religious Idea. All history is the unfolding of this Idea in the world of Man. And the greatest moments of that history are the times when that Idea has triumphed supreme.

Such a view of human life and of its history is, of course, very foreign and utterly strange to modern man, who ordinarily is a citizen of a State where Religion is of the least concern to both the governed and governors.

The modern liberal and democratic states are, in effect, pre-eminently lay states. By proclaiming thus their indifference to the religious phenomenon they have sanctioned in a way the present decay of the religious spirit, that decay so clearly noticeable and so widely deplored throughout the western world.

It is not unusual, in fact, to find words like these expressing the sad state of affairs:

"Religion was once and not so long ago a living, vibrant, all-pervading, all-controlling inner reality, holding unchallenged sovereignty over the purposes, loyalties and conduct of life. . . . Today it is one among the incidental concerns of life. . . ."

The warning that Rudolph Eucken uttered long ago, the warning that along with the downfall of religion, the downfall of all morality is inevitably bound to take place, was never heeded, and after twenty years, it has to be repeated anew in different form by Fascist thinkers. . . .

But, within the State or outside the State, with its co-operation, or without its co-operation, in its pure form, or in a degenerated form, Religion still lives on in the world of man. And that form of State which ignores or under-estimates its vitality and its powerful influence, loses the great help of one of the main moulding forces of the character of its citizens.

Furthermore, were Religion, like Ethics, a phenomenon of the activity of the Spirit entirely independent of any material connection, the supreme indifference of the State in its regard would be, if not justified, at least partially condoned.

But, as it is, all religious activity is connected to manifestations of those intermediary agents of Religion which are called by the generic name of Churches. A church, however, like any other organization of material or spiritual interests, can find its primary reason for existence only in the acquiescence of the State.

And so it happens that when willingly or unwillingly, consciously or unconsciously, the State abdicates its sovereignty, it renders itself at once vulnerable to decay. Nothing will stand, in fact, between a condition of ignorance of its law and one of open rebellion.

The attitude of the State toward the Church or the Churches which are at work in its midst determines thus, in a way, the outcome of a very important issue; namely, can the State abdicate its right to supervision of such a large part of the life of its subjects as their religious life?

The Fascist State firmly and energetically rejects an affirmative answer to such a question. The Fascist State is truly a sovereign State and, as such, arbiter of the fate of the Church, whenever the Church, in the explication of its mission, becomes subject to the authority of social, political or economic laws.

But by recognizing at the outset the high historical function of the Church and by doing whatever is in its power that this function may be fulfilled without hindrance and to the fullest extent of its aims, the Fascist State, which, as we have said, is already an Ethical State, becomes in addition, a Religious State.

"A people cannot become great and powerful," said Mussolini on the 23rd of September, 1924, "cannot become conscious of its high destiny, if it does not value Religion and does not consider it as an essential element of its public and private life."

"No true Society can exist without a common belief and a common aim," Mazzini wrote, "Religion declares the belief and the aim. Politics regulates society in the practical realization of that belief and prepares the means of attaining that aim. Religion represents the principle; politics the application.

"The Religious idea is the very breath of humanity; its life, soul, conscience and manifestation. Humanity exists only in the consciousness of its origin and the presentiment of its destiny; and only reveals itself by concentrating its powers upon someone of the intermediate points between these two. Now this is precisely the function of the religious idea. That idea constitutes a faith in an origin common to us all; sets before us, as a principle, a common future; unites all the active faculties on one sole center, whence they are continuously evolved and developed in the direction of the future, and guides the latent forces of the human mind toward it.

"It lays hold of life in every aspect, and in its

slightest manifestations; utters its augury over the cradle and the tomb, and affords at once the highest and the most universal formula of a given epoch of civilization; the most simple and comprehensive expression of its knowledge (scientia); the ruling synthesis by which it is governed as a whole, and by which its succesive evolutions are directed from on high."

One of the main beliefs forming part of the universal aspects of the Doctrine of Fascism: the belief in the supreme worth of the religious experience, is thus part of the heritage of Mazzini.

Connected with this belief is the other in a transcendent God. There is no place indeed in Fascism for an atheistic conception of the Universe, or for any other conception derived through the analytical powers of the mind.

Fascism holds that the truth about Infinite God cannot be learned by finite Man in any other way than through revealed religion, and that nothing else has contributed so effectively to the present state of chaos of the modern world as the loss of faith in revealed religion.

Furthermore, Fascism holds that in its protean, multiform aspects, life escapes the iron nets of any system of knowledge built up by the sheer powers of reason. Because life breaks through all those categories of thought with the help of which we try to classify and catalogue it, and in the end laughs at us and mocks all our hard-gained and worthless knowledge.

How pitiful indeed, but how true, that life should overwhelm us with its sweeping flood of feelings, instincts, desires, emotions, which we try so vainly to understand, let alone direct or control.

Now it is just this belief of Fascism that no man has ever been able or will ever be able to encompass the whole of life in a rational system of logic, it is just this belief that life is more than reason, that sustains and determines the humble attitude of Fascism toward the great mystery of life and death and the supreme, inscrutable mystery of God.

And, inasmuch as all life issues from God and returns to God, Fascism finds it necessary to cultivate in the growing individual this sense of the intimate relationship between Man and his Maker, so that he may come to realize in the dawn of his spiritual awakening his true place in the visible and the invisible universe.

We must not forget the words of Gentile: "An irreligious State is not a State at all," or the words of Havelock Ellis: "With the passing of the last God and the last Religion the death-knell of man would be rung."

But the Fascist State is not only pre-eminently religious, it is, furthermore, particularly Catholic in thought as well as in experience. And we have come at this point upon another greatly misunderstood attitude of Fascism; namely, its adherence to the Catholic interpretation of Religious experience. This adherence involves another fundamental tenet of the philosophy of Fascism and one of which it is well worth going into further details.

Fascism holds that we are all children of the past.

Past, present, future. These three magic names which conjure to the individual mind the vision of the continuous flow of time, and are represented in the individual's consciousness as separate mo-

ments of his life history, become, in the consciousness of the race, integral parts of one indivisible
phenomenon, integral parts of one timeless spiritual
experience. Because we are all children of the past
and makers of the future.

Out of the depths of time we see the past beckon
to us and remind us that all our institutions, the
home in which we grow to manhood, the school
which makes of us citizens of this world, the church
which teaches us the existence of another and higher
world, are all products of the age-long struggle of
man to raise himself up from the beast.

And, in turn, it is given to us the power and the
glory to bring the weight of our intuitions, our
convictions and our inspirations to bear upon
those same institutions and determine in this way
the very course they shall take in the future.

If it is true, then, as Fascism holds, that we are
all children of the past and that the peculiar heritage of a people is the most precious thing for that
people; if all that is true, then it is also true that
the unbroken tradition of 1900 years of Catholicism cannot be lightly dismissed, but must be held,
rather, as an experience of the Italian race which
is beyond compare in the life of the Spirit.

In the words of Mussolini: "We must never disrupt the continuity of tradition. Traditions constitute a great moral force in the history of people,
and if you eliminate them, you eliminate the foundations on which the history of the future is to be
built, for that history is nothing more than a further achievement and a further perfection of the
past."

And, in the words of Gentile: "The Italian has

always been Catholic in his philosophy; Catholicism has been the very inspiration of his philosophy from Bruno and Campanella, to Vico, Rosmini and Gioberti."

Italian Fascism, therefore, which cannot and will not repudiate such a glorious past, holds that the growing youth of the land must learn that God exists and that the Catholic Church is his Church.

Fascism, which is believed to be the antithesis of spiritual things, is thus the best representative expression of the deep yearning of man for his communion with the Spirit, and, consequently, the truest child of that vision of life which made of Mazzini the champion of Religion in the world of Man.

It is finally of Mazzini also, the Fascist belief in the power and the supremacy of the ideal over the material, that belief which can stop the sun in its course, move the mountains from their beds, unlock the doors of heaven and hell and make of man a martyr or a hero.

"Always love and venerate the Ideal," says Mazzini, "The Ideal is the word of God. High above every country, high above humanity is the country of the Spirit, the city of the Soul, in which all are brethren who believe in the inviolability of thought and in the dignity of our immortal Soul, and the baptism of this fraternity is martyrdom. From that high sphere spring the principles which alone can redeem the people.

"Great ideas create great people. Let your life be the living summary of one organic idea. Enlarge the horizon of the people. Liberate their conscience from the materialism from which it is weighed down. Set a vast mission before them. Re-baptize them. Rekindle faith. Faith which is intellect, energy and love, will put an end to the discords existing in a society which has no leaders; which invokes a new world, but forgets to ask its secret, its word, from God."

Mazzini passes thus through the iridescent landscape of thought which constitutes the background of Fascism as a figure of dynamic moral power. Like a prophet of old, like a biblical Samuel or Elijah, he preaches once again the salvation and regeneration of Man.

His words were addressed to Italy and to the Italians, but they do not belong to one country and only to certain men; they were meant for all men: as part of the universal commonwealth of thought they are truly part of the patrimony of the race.

"Rome is more than a city; Rome is a Universal Idea." —MOMMSEN.

CHAPTER XIV

THE LEGACY OF ROME

The historical continuity of political forms, social organization, religious expression and spiritual aspirations, in the life of the Italian people, which had lasted two thousand years and had been broken only in the last few centuries of servitude to foreigners and their foreign ways of living, has been at last restored by Fascism, which is the direct heir of Roman traditions and of Roman ideals.

Fascism means, in fact, the return to Order, to Authority, to Law; the return to the Roman conception of human Society, conception which those centuries of oblivion could obscure but never efface.

Fascism is, in other words, intimately connected to Rome; its mission is the continuation of the mission of Rome; its heritage is the legacy of Rome.

There are some things Rome symbolized in the golden age of its glory which were and still are of supreme significance to mankind; things of the spirit of an eternal and absolute value which Fascism wants restored to their rightful supremacy.

215

Primary among these things is the organization of the family. The family was conceived by the Romans as fulfilling a dual mission in the world of man; it was both the foundation of the State and the foundation of the individual life. As foundation of the State, the family was an organism whose welfare transcended the welfare of the single members; an organism whose life could not be altered by the will of any single individual; an organism, in other words, of social stability invested with dignity, power and worth.

As foundation of the individual life, the family was the ground for the complete unfoldment of the individual's powers, because outside of the family the Romans could not conceive the existence of a full individual life, or of a life, at any rate, worthy of the attribute of human.

Every other institution the Romans allowed to be changed with the change of times, but the constitution of the family, never: because it was the anchorage of their very life, the adamantine rock on which the continuity of this life rested; the rock which had to resist successfully the onslaughts of the petty, selfish, egotistic claims of the individual. And when the constitution of the family, finally undermined by a thousand years of such onslaughts, did change in effect, that decay of the State which the Romans had foreseen and had tried so successfully to stave off for so long a time, set in at last, bringing in its train the collapse of the whole Roman civilization and the beginning of the Dark Ages.

Rightly, Joseph Chamberlain, the exponent of Teutonic supremacy in the world, wrote in his monumental work, "The foundations of Nineteenth Century," "I do not think that any unprejudiced man will deny that the Roman family is one of the most glorious achievements of the human mind, one of those heights which cannot be scaled twice, and to which the most distant generations will look up in admiration, making sure at the same time that they themselves are not straying too far from the right path."

But the Roman conception of the family has been long neglected and this neglect Fascism holds to be one of the main causes of the present moral decadence and social unrest.

Thus we find Fascism, once more going to the root of one of the great evils of modern life, re-attach itself to the Roman tradition and restore the meaning and the importance of the family as builder of the soul and foundation of the State.

All that contributes to the strengthening of the structure of the family, all that binds family ties still closer, all that promotes the growth of that unique atmosphere of the family where the purest, the noblest, the greatest relationships are born and developed, all that enhances the blossoming and the flowering of the heart's deepest loves, all that, and nothing else, is good.

All that which would tend to disintegrate the social structure, which would accelerate that process of dissolution of all human institutions, so clearly apparent in modern life; all that, in fine, which would bring man back to a dangerous state of unrestrained license, is evil.

The function of the Fascist State is, therefore, clearly defined as that of the staunchest supporter of the family; the enlargement of the social scope and activity of the family group are all parts of a progressive and very effective program of rebuilding and rehabilitation of the family in the Fascist State.

Finally, it is a fundamental thought behind Fascist activity that all of man's conquests over the external world, all of the ingenuous tools and amazing devices are merely dead things which cannot and will never satisfy the deepest yearning of man. That yearning is to love and to be loved. And because to love and to be loved is truly the essence of life, Fascism believes with Mazzini that: "The family is the fatherland of the heart." Undoubtedly, the family has other functions beside that described by the poetic words of Mazzini, but if the true nature of man is that of a being to whom whatever speaks of the heart is dear, then it is true also that whatever rightfully belongs to the heart must receive paramount consideration in the planning of his social structure. Thus we find that Fascism, convinced that all other considerations fade in significance and importance when contrasted with that primary and most excellent one, is rebuilding that temple where first and last the human heart learns of love and, in so doing, is re-establishing the continuity of the Roman tradition in the world of man.

But the continuity of the Roman tradition is not fulfilled only by the translation into a fact of the conception of the role played by the family in the individual and social life of man.

A far greater conception forms indeed the background of that Universal Idea which is the Idea of Rome. That conception is the conception of Empire as the only unifying principle of all mankind.

Empire, in the generally accepted meaning, is a political organization whose foundation is always a territorial extension. Empire, in the Fascist meaning of the word denotes, instead, that unification of peoples and nations brought about by the triumph of a universal idea. Hence, the seat of Empire is necessarily there where the realization of this universal Idea takes place.

It is not incomprehensible, thus, that Rome has been twice the seat of Empire, and that she has been chosen again by destiny to fill such a role for the third successive time in the twenty-eighth century of her fateful history.

Twice in the past, from Rome, a Universal Idea has sent a message of harmony and unity to divided, warring and ailing mankind. Twice have the seven hills of Rome seen the triumph of this Idea bring about in their midst the realization of Empire.

The triumph of the Idea of Order, of Authority, of equal Justice under Law, saw the Empire of Augustus and of Trajanus give to mankind for the first and only time in human history the life-enhancing blessing of political unity.

The triumph of the Catholic Idea of salvation in Christ and through Christ and His Church, saw the Empire of the Church give to mankind the life-inspiring blessing of spiritual unity.

The triumph of the Fascist Idea of subjection of all individual life to the life of the Whole will see a new Empire rise on the seven hills of Rome, an empire founded not necessarily upon territorial possessions and political conquests, but primarily upon the generalized belief that Fascism may finally furnish man with the long sought solution of the riddle of life.

A spiritual power generated from those great Italian spirits who have been in the past the assertors of Rome's immortal and eternal right to Empire, and the prophets of Rome's third form of Empire, is the leaven which has brought about that fermentation of spiritual forces called Fascism.

We have already said that Fascism as a system of thought is not the offspring of a hastily concocted and hardly digested body of ideas. It is rather the direct, lineal descendant of a whole historical, philosophical tradition which remounts through the centuries toward the greatest thinker of Italy, connecting thus in an indissoluble unity the past to the present, what was prophesied then with what has been accomplished now.

Dante has been called, and is commonly held to be, "the spokesman of the Middle Ages." And in a certain sense he was. But what matters most to Italy and to Italians: Dante is the precursor of modern Italy, or, more exactly, he is the apostle of those ideas and those beliefs which have become articles of faith of the Fascist creed, and, in particular, of the concept of Empire which plays one of the leading roles in the Fascist philosophy of life.

Everybody knows the "Divine Comedy." Very few, however, know the existence of such works of Dante as the "Vita Nuova," the "Convivio" and the "De Monarchia."

But the full import of the message delivered by the "Divine Comedy" can never be understood and appreciated in its full measure unless it is approached through a study of his minor works. Minor, that is, in relation to the vastness and the magnificence of the "Divine Comedy," but, in themselves, works of the highest philosophical importance.

In "Vita Nuova" Dante teaches man never to despair of life, never to doubt the immortality of the soul, and never to forget that the love of man is a parcel of the divine love, because Man issues from God and returns to God.

In "Convivio" Dante teaches man that Humanity is one and that this unity requires a common spiritual center as the rallying focus of the spiritual energies of the race and as the cementing factor of all diversities, all aspirations, all ambitions. In the "Convivio" Dante has the first vision of the Empire as "The Universal Religion of Human Nature," that vision which constitutes the essence of "De Monarchia."

It has been said by some well meaning but ill informed critics that "De Monarchia" is nothing more than a political treatise of the Middle Ages, and that, consequently, the ideas expounded therein are impossible of application in our modern times. It remains, instead, the greatest glory of Dante that his message is a message of all times, capable of application then as well as now, and whenever man comes to the realization of those fundamental truths which form the very web of life.

A profound religious outlook informs and characterizes the whole book of "De Monarchia;" a religious outlook not sectarian but of the widest understanding of and sympathy for, the will of God; that will which, adequately realized in the world of man, demands that mankind must be one, even as God is one; one in organization as it is already one in principle.

To bring about such a realization, a universal empire must come into being, an empire subject to the lordship of a sole Monarch. Then, and only then, man will find peace, that peace which is the primary condition of the good life; that peace which alone can make possible for him to fulfill his destiny.

And because the mission of Rome through the ages has been a mission of spiritual focus for the whole world, Dante shows that nowhere else can the seat of Empire be than in Rome; Rome, the city predilect of the Gods, untouched by death, hallowed by time.

And, finally, because in Rome rest both the seat of the temporal power in the Monarchy and the seat of the spiritual power in the Papacy, Dante, with a truly prophetic insight, shows how the two powers can co-exist without being at war with each other, as the two poles of being of a dual organization realizing the will of God in the world of man.

It is the message of Dante delivered separately in "Vita Nuova," in "Convivio" and in "De Monarchia," and in one magnificent harmony in the "Divine Comedy," which is the inspiration and the leaven of the life of Fascist Italy. It is the thought Dante — "Dante, deep, fierce, the central fire of the world" — striving for realization after a sad interval of six centuries, which is the background of Fascism and imparts to it its universal and timeless appeal.

And if ever man can be inspired by one of his fellow-beings, it is Dante who can inspire him be-

222

cause in no other human creature, at any time of human history, have all the faculties of the soul found such a complete and perfect expression as they did in him. Truly Dante is "The Hero of the Soul."

Intimately linked to the thought of Dante is the thought of Vincenzo Gioberti, a great figure of the Italian "Risorgimento," another great apostle of modern Italy and another prophet of Italy's, third Empire.

The message of Gioberti is the message of Dante delivered with a new voice, a new accent and new words.

"Del Primato morale e civile degli Italiani," (On the Moral and Civil Primacy of the Italian people) is one of those books which leave an indelible mark upon the soul of a nation.

But to call the Primato a book is not quite correct, because it is something more than a mere book; it is a message; it is a call and a prophecy. Nowhere else have the claims of Italy and of the Italians to supreme primacy in the moral and social realms — apart from the "De Monarchia" of Dante, which establishes and supports these claims in the political field — found such forceful and thorough expression as in the two large volumes of the Primato.

The main thesis of the Primato is that modern Civilization is built and must rest upon the foundations laid by Christianity and that the true expression of Christianity is found only in Catholicism.

"European Civilization must be re-established a second time by recalling it to its Christian and Catholic origins and extinguishing the heterodoxy which for two centuries reigned in all its parts. . . .

When a civilization is to be rebuilt, a moral center of action must be established where the source of motion may reside and whence the movement may be spread to all its parts as from the center to the circumference.

"History teaches that every civilization has its special seat in one country or city as its base, which becomes morally the capital of the civilized world.

"The center of the civilizing process is where the center of Catholicism is. . . . Now, since Italy is center of the latter, it follows that Italy is the true head of civilization and Rome the ideal metropolis of the world.

"Providence chose the Italian land for this high destiny, nourishing a spark of divine truth in it "ab antico" and molding there a race wonderfully adapted in genius and intelligence for subjecting the whole world in Christian obedience. . . . Italy is the priestly nation among the great body of redeemed peoples. . . . Nor did the inhabitants of this peninsula give to other peoples merely divine gifts, but also every other civil and human good, and all the great intellects of Europe, who enhanced in any measure the glory of their countries, lit their lamps at the living flame of Italian genius."

Words like these are words of fire, and very little wonder is left, after reading them, at the vision of Italy dreaming once more dreams of glory, dreams of greatness, dreams of empire.

"I picture to myself the rejoicing and the elation of the sea when Italian fleets will go sailing again upon its unbounded domains and when it will see itself return again under the power of that strong and generous race, which once gave to it its names.

"I see in the future the eyes of Europe focused upon the re-born Italy; I see all the other nations, diffident at first, then receptive and anxious, receive from her the principles of truth, the form of beauty, the example of the moral life, the law of justice."

Strange, prophetic words uttered in one of the darkest periods of Italian history, when it was treason to dream of a better Italy, when it was hopeless to dream of independence and liberty, and nothing else was left to the Italian nation than black, profound despair.

But these words remained to gather dust on the shelves of libraries through a whole century; they remained dead words until the day that Fascism discovered that the thought of Gioberti was its own thought, that the spirit of Gioberti was its own spirit, that the vision of Gioberti was its own vision.

The imperialism preached by Dante and by Gioberti found its first adequate expression as integral part of Fascism in the article of Mussolini in "Popolo d'Italia," of September 15, 1919.

"Imperialism is the eternal and immutable law of life," Mussolini wrote, "At bottom it is but the need, the desire and the will for expansion which every living, healthy individual or people has in itself. It is the means by which it is practiced that distinguishes one imperialism from another, both among individuals and among peoples."

What is important to notice now is not this belief of the immanence of imperialism in the life of man, but the belief expressed by the words which follow; namely, the belief in a spiritual possibility of imperialism. It is this possibility dimly seen in

1919 which becomes a certainty and the very essence of imperialism a few years later.

"Imperialism is not necessarily, as is commonly believed, aristocratic and military. Imperialism may be democratic, pacific, economic or spiritual."

These are Mussolini's words of 1919. But six years later, when he treats again of the imperialistic theme, he stops to consider empire as being first of all and above all a triumph of the Spirit. ". . . the goal is always: Empire! To build a city, to found a colony, to establish an empire, these are the prodigies of the human spirit."

Imperialism, this element of Fascism which represents one of the multiform facets of its variegated structure, becomes thus another means by which the Spirit strives for expression in the life of man.

This belief of Fascism in the essential spirituality of the nature of man is a revelation of the existence of an esoteric aspect of Fascism, that aspect which is concerned mainly with the development of man's spiritual nature and alone has meaning and value for the whole world of man.

It is, therefore, something more than a singular coincidence that the philosopher of Fascism is the Philosopher of the Spirit.

To no other mind of modern times has, in fact, the revelation of the immanence of the Spirit in the life of Man appeared so certain, so evident, and so irrefutable, as to the mind of Giovanni Gentile.

Through Giovanni Gentile Fascism re-affirms its belief that the Spirit, always present, always active, always at work within the life of Man, confers to this life a meaning, a purpose and a dignity, which fully justify the whole historical process through

226

which Man rises by degrees to the vision and the realization of the good life; that life which feeds on Heroism and has Empire as its goal.

CHAPTER XV

DUX

THE HERO AS LEADER

In this skeptical, faithless and unbelieving age it will undoubtedly appear as a most preposterous and ridiculous attempt to provide a continuation of Carlyle's lectures on "Heroes and Hero-Worship," by adding a seventh one on the Hero as Leader, to his original and incomparable six.

The age of hero-worship appears to us most strange and remote, indeed; the very possibility of a hero appearing in our midst is denied with a vehemence and a finality which reveal our incapacity to understand the true essence of heroism; everything points, in other words, to the low state to which has fallen the cult and the practice of the heroic in man.

But if the age of hero-worship is past forever, it is not true that heroes may not appear in our midst.

What is a Hero, the Carlylean Hero?

A hero is he who can pierce with the mystic light

229

of an inner vision to the very heart of things; he who can re-discover the greatest and most profound of all truths: viz., that beyond this realm of fugitive appearances there lies, immutable and eternal, what Fichte called the "Divine Idea of the World;" finally, he who, living already in spirit in this realm of timeless and absolute Reality, is able to translate his vision into deeds and to act according to the dictates of an inner voice telling him that ". . . they wrong man greatly who say he is to be seduced by ease. Difficulty, abnegation, martyrdom, death are the allurements that act on the heart of man."

As a god or a prophet, as a saint or a warrior, as a poet or a king; under whatever aspect they might have appeared on this earth, all heroes have always delivered and, for that matter, will ever deliver, the same message to mankind: viz., that man lives a true human life only when his life is devoted to and, if necessary, sacrificed for the triumph of an ideal and that only by living such a life can he ever find happiness on this earth.

And because every age brings forth its own type of hero, the Hero as Leader; the new type of hero born of the need of the times, answering the call of history, in delivering anew such a message—a message of hope and trust, of faith and revolt, of abnegation and assertion at the same time—must deliver it not in the form of revealed religion, not in the form of a God-inspired book, of a prophecy, or of a poem encompassing earth and heaven, but in the form of a new way of life: a way of life capable of leading man out of his present unhappy, miserable state.

230

The Hero as Leader!

To acknowledge that a man in our midst, a man of flesh and bone, with our vices and our virtues, with our strength and our weaknesses, with our aspirations and our dreams, is truly a Hero: the Hero as Leader, we must ask of him first of all, and above all, that through his speech, his actions, his influence, his example, his whole life, in short, he live the very message he is delivering to us.

But this is not sufficient; we want to be certain that he is not a quack, a charlatan or an impostor, but a true and sincere man. Sincerity of purpose, that magic touchstone which serves so well to distinguish the gold from the dross in the actions of men—is what we expect to find in the man to be recognized as hero.

And yet, sincerity, however admirable it may be, by itself achieves nothing everlasting if it is not accompanied by courage. Nothing great, nothing of any value, of any meaning whatsoever can ever be accomplished in this world of ours, if all fear of the known and unknown hostile, belittling or derisive forces is not banished from the heart and the mind of man.

Finally, sincerity and courage must be accompanied by belief; belief in one's own destiny, belief in the role which one is destined to play on the stage of life, belief in one's own powers if the world is to be actually and effectively changed through one's own efforts.

Underlying this magic trinity of sincerity, courage and faith, there must always exist within the soul's deepest recesses a mystic power of immediate knowledge of the truth through the supreme gift of intuition, if the action of a man must share the finality of an act of God.

Once we find all these qualities within the soul of one man, once we discover that they not only exist there, but have taken complete possession of his inner life, blotting out—so to speak—any other virtue, any other vice, then we may rest assured that we have found a man entitled to our admiration, a true hero worthy of inclusion within the sacred cohort of the Carlylean heroes.

But our skeptical brethren—little men without vision, without faith, without belief—ask for pragmatic proof of his right to our admiration, if not to our worship. Such proof is evidently not needed by those who can recognize The Hero when they see him, but is sorely needed by those aware of the bread they eat but blind to the reality of the unseen.

To this category of people, condemned by a mean fate to the worst form of cecity of all, it will be necessary to furnish explanations, it will be necessary to ask them whether an impostor, a quack, a false man could ever bring about the unification of a nation, the resurrection of an empire, the redemption of a land, the regeneration of the moral conscience of a people. What impostor, what quack, what false man has ever accomplished that before? By what miracle of ingenuity, cunning or malice, has he ever been able to fool all the people all of the time? And is that ever possible?

If what was accomplished once is guaranty of what can be accomplished now, if the past is forerunner of the present, if it is true that "Historia magistra vitae," we are forced to acknowledge then that there is here among us on this earth a man

232

marked by Destiny to say a new word to mankind. His words, his deeds, his thoughts, the whole life of this man is a living lesson of heroism for all those timid souls who believe that there is no greater thing on earth than to be satisfied with a routine, commonplace existence.

How deeply, movingly pathetic beyond words it is to see this man, burning with the great flame that he has carried and still carries, deep within; seek here and there and everywhere a refuge, and with the refuge a piece of bread, and with the piece of bread the means to bring forth that inner flame burning deep, deep within. How inspiring to see him follow the call of destiny without being aware of exactly what destiny expected from him; only dimly perceiving in a blurred vision the image of some great thing shaping itself in the mist, and calling to him, leading him, drawing him toward an unknown and perhaps dangerous goal.

Does the light point to socialism, Marxist utopia, class struggle, international brotherhood?

Through long years of struggle, sacrifices, privations, sorrows, he gives all of himself to the triumph of those mirages; for the triumph of socialism, Marxist utopia, class struggle, international brotherhood, he lives and is always ready to die.

Alas, what a bitter taste have the fruits of victory! Victory means, in effect, nothing less than the nullification of all the work, all the sufferances, all the martyrdom of the patriots who made Italy one again after centuries of dismemberment, serfdom and abjection.

But the hour of destiny is calling. Is there no hope left for Italy? Must Italy renounce forever

233

to her glorious past? Must she resign herself to a
minor role in world history? Is there no significance
in all that which forms the substance of the Idea
of a nation, the Italian nation? Was the exile of
Mazzini, the imprisonment of Pellico, the death of
Menotti, the martyrdom of Mameli, the holocaust
of the Bandieras, the heroism of Garibaldi, all a
mistake? Was the blood shed to make of Italy a
nation again, shed all in vain? Were the hours of
anxiety of Cavour, the vision of Gioberti, the work
of Victor Emmanuel, all fruits of a great joke of
some devilish power?

Questions like these must have agitated the mind
and the heart of that man when the hour of destiny
struck its call.

But the mist enveloping the vision haunting his
dreams since the early days of his youth is finally
lifting, the contours of this vision become finally
sharp, clear and distinct. . . . What do they reveal
to the inner eye of the seer? They reveal the image
of the great mother Italy sunk in the mire, seeking
light, pleading for help.

It was then that a true, complete revolution of
all thoughts, all feelings, all sensations, took the soul
of that man by storm and forced him to examine
critically his whole past, revise all his beliefs, fashion
for himself a new creed, find within himself the
capacity to utter a new word, the WORD that a
whole people, a whole continent, the whole western
civilization was in need to hear and was waiting
to hear.

He had then the intuition that something of tre-
mendous import for mankind was at stake, hung
precariously on the decision of his life course; he

had the revelation that an issue of far-reaching consequence for the future of mankind had to be settled then. It was a question whether, faced by the decay of the liberal-democratic-capitalistic-materialistic organization of society, man had to embrace communism and abjection or choose another way of life in tune with his soul's aspirations, if not with his animal nature's wants.

It was thus that the dumb, inchoate historical forces which shape the destinies of man found suddenly a voice; it was thus that centuries of thought and action were brought suddenly to a climax by such a voice; it was thus that the people themselves acquired suddenly the voice they so earnestly and yet so vainly had sought; because if Fascism is a creature of the man Benito Mussolini, yet, in truth, it belongs to western civilization itself.

The man was simply the mouthpiece chosen by destiny to utter what needed to be uttered at a crucial time of human history; what he said all people were longing to say; what he did many people, perhaps, were trying to do.

He actually expressed in words what remained unexpressed in the inmost heart of the people; he only translated into action what lay dormant in a potential state within the very nature of the people.

Alone, he could achieve nothing. As a leader he could change, and is changing the aspect of the world.

We must never forget that—as we have already said and shall again repeat—it was the fact that the soil was ready for the sowing of his message; it was the dire need that such a message should be delivered; it was, finally, the decline of a whole civilization that made possible the triumph of Fascism.

Thus it always happens in human affairs—"Even that which is greater," says Rudolph Eucken, "has its necessary presuppositions and conditions; the soil must be ready, the age must contribute the stimulus of its special problems."

The only merit of Mussolini, the truly great merit of this man, is that he took up the challenge of communism and he *dared*, and in daring he has given to the world the incomparable gift of a new type of life: a type of life which places heroism, asceticism, martyrdom and death above comfort, cowardice, safety and well being: a type of life acknowledging the unity which is at the root of life, stressing the invisible tie which binds together the destinies of all men: a type of life which recognizes the need of man's worship of those intangible things called the Ideals of the Fatherland, the State, the Church and the Family: a type of life finally in which Authority, Responsibility and Duty take the place of that negative form of Liberty which is the anathema of the only form of Liberty worth living and dying for—the Liberty of the Spirit.

In so doing; in offering to the people hardships, sufferings, privations and wants in place of ease, comfort, abundance and riches, Mussolini is fulfilling the prophecies of all the great souls of the nineteenth century who preached the new way of life but found none who could translate it into fact.

He is fulfilling, for instance, the prophecy of Nietzsche who in an age sick with all the diseases of the soul, rises like a prophet of old to preach the heroic life, the dangerous life, the ascetic life, the

236

spiritual life; of Nietzsche who in an age resounding with the battle-cry of Democracy disdainfully remarks: "Once the Spirit was God; then it became Man, and now it even becometh Populace;" of Nietzsche who in an age replete with hypocrisy, false pretences and make-believe, let Zarathustra wander through the world to announce the true life, the sincere life, the genuine life; of Nietzsche, finally, who in an age which believes that the most desirable aim of human life is to live according to Nature, has the courage to say: "Imagine to yourselves a being like Nature, boundlessly extravagant, boundlessly indifferent, without purpose or consideration, without pity or justice, at once fruitful and barren and uncertain: imagine to yourselves *Indifference* as a power—how could you live in accordance with such indifference? To live—is not that just endeavoring to be otherwise than this Nature? Is not living: valuing, preferring, being unjust, being limited, endeavoring to be different?" He is fulfilling also the words of Carlyle—"Belief is great, life-giving. The history of a nation becomes fruitful, soul-elevating, great, so soon as it believes."

He is letting mankind acknowledge the truth already seen by Emerson in his mystic moments of supreme intuition, the truth that, "What we commonly call man: the eating, drinking, planting, counting man, does not, as we know him, represent himself, but misrepresents himself," or, as Carlyle puts it: "They wrong man greatly who say he is to be seduced by ease. Difficulty, abnegation, martyrdom, death, are the allurements that act on the heart of man. Kindle the inner genial life of him,

237

you have a flame that burns up all lower consideration."

He is letting the words of Alfredo Oriani, the solitary thinker of the coming age of man, be the guide of his attitude toward the new aristocracy of Fascism: "Aristocracy is immortal!"

"That superiority which is basis of the aristocratic character has its origin within the very nature of the individuals: it shows itself as a characteristic which makes them different from the crowd and leads them to associate themselves, to establish an hierarchical arrangement among themselves, and to give unity to their work and immortality to their Kind."

He is fulfilling finally the prophecies of all the forerunners of Fascism, from Vico to Mazzini, from Dante to Gioberti, from Carlyle to Carducci; he is letting all the words of those great souls who believed in the power and the beauty of the Ideal become fact, by making the people accept them as the gospel of a new way of life, by making the people believe in them, work for them, suffer for them, die for them.

Truly, if any man is entitled to be called Hero, that man certainly is: a new type of Hero, the Hero of the times, the Hero as Leader.

"Ideals are not fully themselves until they are transmuted into forces." —CROCE.

CHAPTER XVI

THE FASCIST REVOLUTION

"My individuality is the totality of social relations."

These few words of Karl Marx, from his "Communist Manifesto" published in 1846, are the right and necessary prolegomena to a summary description of the Fascist Revolution.

The Fascist Revolution is at bottom a revolution against the men, the ideas and the conditions which let the individual's consciousness of the self begin and end with the limits of the individual's personality.

It is true that Karl Marx, when he wrote those words, had in mind a different type of revolution coming to break the boundaries of individuality than the Fascist one; but it is also true that there is not one way alone to solve the eternal problem of the right relationship of Individual versus Society and that the Communist way is certainly not the way of the western world.

A fundamental characteristic of the culture of

239

the western world has always been the emphasis placed on the free activity of the human spirit as prime mover of the forces shaping the course of human history.

A fundamental characteristic of the Communist way is, instead, the emphasis placed on materialistic historic determinism, as the true agent conditioning the aspects and the development of human life.

By restricting the motives of human actions to economic motives only, by further restricting these economic motives to class struggle, Karl Marx was able to state: "The history of all hitherto existing societies is the history of class struggle."

Destroy all economic inequality, eliminate the economic exploitation of one class by another, bring about the rise of the proletarian class to the pre-eminent position in the social structure, instaurate the communist society; you have perfected then, according to the prophets of communism, all individual and social life.

Such a materialistic interpretation of human history, based on an economic determinism conditioning the actions and the purposes of men, Fascism definitely and vigorously rejects.

Fascism holds that it is not through the triumph of one class at the expense of the others; it is not through the abolition of inequality of economic and material conditions; it is not through the furthering of all edonistic goals, that the true way may be found to break the iron-clad defenses built by the modern individual at the boundaries of his personality.

A different method of attack has to be devised. Equality of income will never satisfy the supreme aspirations of man. Elimination of the war of classes through the enslavement of all other classes to the proletarian masters can bring forth only more chaos, unhappiness and despair. Other means must be found. . . .

Destroy obsolete institutions, educate the people to see higher things in life than materialistic aims, organize society on a basis of co-operation, hierarchy and harmony, let an élite of aristocratic spirits lead society onward, let the goal of man be to achieve spiritual greatness, not wealth; these are the means which the Fascist Revolution has found and is attempting to use.

The Fascist Revolution, which is none the less a revolution because its aims are being achieved peacefully, has only begun. Its course will extend perhaps over the whole span of the twentieth century. It certainly is not going to end before the final debacle of Individualism and its offspring.

"A Revolution," said Mazzini, "is the passage of an Idea from theory to practice." The Fascist Revolution will have completed its course only when the cardinal Idea lying at its base has become a reality of everyday life; when the common man will acknowledge that his individuality does not stop at the boundaries of his personality, but includes "the totality of social relations."

It is to make such realization possible that the Fascist Revolution has devised such radical means as the destruction of all obsolete institutions.

Of all obsolete institutions, the capitalist system is the most obsolete of all.

A series of destructive forces has made of it such an anachronistic thing in our times and in our form of society that no human effort will ever be able to salvage it.

The first destructive force originates within the system itself from the contradiction existing between the fact that the capitalist system is a *social* organism of production and the purpose of men is to make of it an *individual* means of personal profit.

The second is a force originated by those outside agents called machines, which, displacing human labor, can create a surplus of commodities without creating the means for disposing of it; that is, without correspondingly increasing, but, rather, actually decreasing the number of salaried workers needed for the production and the consumption of these commodities.

The third is a force originated by the sad truth that capitalism can thrive only through the exploitation of the many of the few; a force, therefore, eminently anti-social and retrogressive.

Finally, the growth of large trusts and monopolies, of absentee ownership of the factors of production, of organizations requiring ever expanding markets for the continuity of their existence, of economic private interests conflicting with the wider interests of the nation as a whole, and of an international fraternity controlling the destinies of men and nations alike, completes the series of destructive forces which have made of the capitalist system the most obsolete thing of our days.

First and foremost to be abolished, therefore, is the capitalist structure, or, rather, the capitalist super-structure which has done such great harm to modern society.

But the doom of Capitalism brings about in its

train the doom of Democracy, because the obsolete aspect of the one is intimately related to the obsolete aspect of the other.

It has been said many times, indeed, and it must be here repeated again, that Democracy can thrive only in a society composed of economically free individuals.

Such a type of society may have existed once; but it certainly does not exist nowadays. Capitalism has succeeded, within the brief span of a century of time, in destroying its very possibility of realization.

When the progressive disintegration of the capitalist system gives birth to the strange phenomenon of vast accumulations of products facing vast hordes of starving men who are not entitled to the consumption of those products which are destroyed instead of distributed, the time is well nigh at hand that the word Democracy has lost all meaning. What meaning can Democracy have for the masses, when the rights of free speech, free vote, free press, have become ghastly parodies of the very right to life?

But even assuming that the impossible may happen, that the process of history may be reversed, that society may revert to that stage of life when universal distribution of wealth, individually owned means of production, small accumulations of capital and equal economic advantages under a true system of free competition may make actually possible the realization of Democracy; is it not sadly true that the final effect of Democracy on human life is a levelling tendency, resulting in a uniformity of ideas, of institutions, of habits, of laws, which in the end would kill all originality, all individuality, all moral and spiritual greatness?

It is exactly this vision of the incompatibility of such obsolete institutions as Capitalism and Democracy with the present conditions of Society, the vision that led Karl Marx to prophesy the coming Revolution: the Communist Revolution, as the only means of escape from the collapse of the social order.

Little did Karl Marx dream that there was another way of escape than the way of the proletariat's triumph; that other means than the Communist means could be found to bring about the birth of a new social order.

Little did Karl Marx foresee the coming Fascist Revolution: the revolution which is now in full swing and of which our children's children will see, perhaps its complete triumph.

Striking at the root of all that which forms the ideologic background of our everyday life, the Fascist Revolution is bringing about in our own times, and while we are only partially aware of it, the most momentous change which ever took place at one time in any period of human history.

The Fascist Revolution has not come to bring about the long sought materialization of Utopia on this earth; it has not come to realize fanciful and fantastic theories within the social organism.

The Fascist Revolution was started and is now in progress for the furtherance of one aim: the realization of a new social order founded on everlasting, life-inspiring Ideals.

The Fascist Revolution is teaching us that human history is more than the story of class struggle; it is teaching us also that there is a way to end the war of classes and that this way is found in placing all classes under the protection, the aegis, and the discipline of the State.

The Fascist Revolution is teaching us that exploitation of one class by another is not compatible with social justice and must be replaced, therefore, by co-operation of the various classes for their own good and for the good of the nation as a whole.

The Fascist Revlution is teaching us that inasmuch as production is national in character, all surplus value derived from the play of productive forces has a national significance and importance, and must not be used, therefore, to enrich private individuals, and further the ends of private interests.

The Fascist Revolution is teaching us that the times cry out aloud for a thorough revision of the principles of production; it is teaching us that there must be national planning, not individual planning of the amount of things produced, and that, furthermore, there must be national planning of its distribution and apportioning among the various classes of society.

Finally, if in the realm of Economics it announces the doom of Capitalism, the Fascist Revolution cannot fail at the same time to express itself as a revolt against all the other aspects of Individualism in the life of man.

The Fascist Revolution is thus a revolt against Liberalism in social theory and social practice, against Democracy in politics, against Materialism and its derivatives in philosophy.

But a revolution is always something more than a revolt.

A revolt can destroy; it cannot build.

A revolution instead creates always new values, is always a fruitful harbinger of a new order of things.

"A religion or a philosophy lies at the base of every revolution," said Mazzini.

The idealistic philosophy which lies at the base of the Fascist Revolution makes of it something more than a revolt, something constructive, creative, spiritual.

It is this idealistic philosophy which is responsible for the realization of the Corporative system replacing the now so utterly obsolete Capitalistic system; which is responsible for that hierarchical organization of society replacing the miserably antiquated Democratic organization; which is responsible for the gospel of Duty as basis of social life, and the gospel of asceticism and heroism as basis of individual life.

To achieve that stage of life where we can confidently state that we have been able to merge our individuality within the social organism, to achieve it through hard struggle, to achieve it against our own will, to suffer gladly misery, martyrdom and death for its sake; that is the teaching, the puropse and the goal of the Fascist Revolution.

CONCLUSION

In a world moving slowly but surely and steadfastly toward a stage of life in which the emphasis placed on human personality will be shifted from the single individual to mankind as a whole; in a world which is slowly but undeniably being transformed by biological, psychological, social and mystical forces from a complex state of chaotic, dissociated, conflicting purposes, to a world of harmonious aims inspired and guided by a common will; in a world, finally, where everything points to an evolution of man from an autonomous animal being to a cell of a moral and spiritual universe; there is no room any longer for that philosophy of life which enjoys the appellative of Individualism.

The perpetuation of such a philosophy can only retard the progress of man toward the final goal of his self-effacement, self-realization and self-identification into the more comprehensive aspects of Reality.

If the final goal of life is, in other words, the spiritualization of man, that philosophic doctrine which teaches human beings to assert their individuality and cherish it as their most precious possession, represents, without doubt, a historical anachronism. Nay, more, such a philosophic doctrine must be held as evil itself and begetter of evils, and must be replaced by a way of life more in tune with the spirit of the times and the needs of the race; a way of life stressing the true virtues of fellowship, co-operation, duty, charity, devotion and love, and obliterating the false ones of selfishness, assertiveness, right, greed, contempt and hate on which mankind has been fed so far, which formed the very spiritual food of our youth and are being taught to our own children on this very day and at this very hour.

Is Fascism the new way of life?

To the reader the answer—

But let the reader be reminded that in answering that question he must not think of the particular, local, transient and narrow aspects that Fascism has assumed in some particular land, but of those timeless, universal, deep aspects of Fascism which alone have meaning and value for the whole world of man and gleam now at the horizon as the only source of light in our otherwise darkened, harassed, struggling and floundering society.

APPENDIX

FASCISM AND AMERICA

It always has been commonly held that the foundations of the United States of America rest upon the subsoil of individualism, and that if the structure of its particular form of democracy should weaken, the very life of the republic would be endangered.

This way of looking superficially into phenomena of such transcendent meaning as the rise of a nation, the development of a culture, the evolution of social formations, the birth of a new civilization, etc., brings about a distrust for formulae and theories born of a deeper insight into the true nature of things.

Were we, in fact, to be told today that the American nation will go on living, growing, evolving, even if its social structure and its political organization followed no longer the pattern of democracy, or if its philosophy of rugged individualism should give place to a new philosophy of life more in tune with the spirit of the times, we would probably deride the suggestion as utterly ridiculous and senseless.

And yet, it remains nevertheless an uncontested truth that the Idea of a nation — what constitutes its essence, what represents it in that realm where appearance fades and reality only reigns supreme — that intangible spirit giving life, unity, and meaning to the otherwise chaotic and meaningless expression of activity of a people, is not and cannot be contingent upon the concourse of outward circumstances, but must needs enjoy an existence of its own, timeless and absolute.

If the American nation is truly a nation at all: that is, if the amalgama of races which have gone into the make-up of its population is to be unified into a living unity with one purpose, one ideal, one duty; if the land on which this population is born and develops has a soul of its own which can germinate through the souls of the individual beings, conferring upon them those intangible characteristics which are the national traits; if finally, the role that the American nation is to play is a role of world-wide significance, then there is no doubt that the American nation will live through the ages regardless of the rise and fall of Fascism, Individualism, Democracy, Liberalism, etc.

But if the American nation is only the shadow of an empty shell, a form without substance, maintained upright by external proppings and paraphernalia, then it is also true that the fall of one of these proppings, the defection of one element of that paraphernalia, would be enough to involve the collapse of the nation as a whole and its return to a state of indistinct chaos.

Before being terrorized thus by the changes involved into the acceptance of the principles of Fascism, let us get rid of our baseless fear, because it might even happen that Fascism — as a philosophy and a way of life — may be the only remedy for our apparently incurable ills and evils.

If we want to be true to ourselves we must begin to confess that in those things which form the true core of Fascism we are sorely deficient and direly in need.

We are in need, in other words, of unselfish love, respect for other beings, consideration for poverty, recognition of authority, admiration for old age, attachment to the hearth, love for the soil, passion for art, devotion to ideals, sacrifices for the common weal: of all things, finally, which are born of the Soul and partake of the Spirit.

Fascism — in its purest and truest expression — is nothing more than what we have not and what, instead, we should have with us and within us if we want to retain any aspiration of a truly civilized nation.

To merge our triumphant individualism in the flood of the great stream of the energies of countless beings, to become part of a great whole, to forsake the claims of our little ego for the larger claims of mankind, to work not for ourselves alone, but for our brethren as well, to realize that we are but small units of a thing greater than ourselves — the nation of which we are part, to have a sense of the littleness of our role and the greatness of the role which the nation is called to play on the stage of life, to acknowledge, finally, that one invisible tie binds together the destinies of all men, such is

Fascism, or, at any rate, such are the elements of Fascism which can become part of our life.

America can have no use for the local, transient aspects and outward forms of Fascism peculiar to the land and of the times in which it had its birth: forms and aspects devoid of universal application and belittling the true spirit of Fascism.

There is not, and there cannot be, any place in America for dictatorship, regimentation, militarism, etc., if this country has to retain through the ages its mission among the nations of the world.

And how truly symbolic is this mission indeed!

Was America not chosen by destiny to become the stage for the last act of the everlasting drama enacted by the common man for the assertion of his rights and the practice of his liberties?

Was America not chosen by destiny to be the great field of unbond opportunities for a freer, a better, a fuller life of the common man?

Was America not chosen by destiny to see the triumph, and be the prize, of the common man's struggle for self-expression, for power, for wealth?

When the common man, who had finally broken the yoke of despotism, tyranny and feudalism only a few centuries before, came to the shores of America, a dream took shape within the deepest recesses of his consciousness: the dream of realizing for once on this earth a blessed state of society in which the rights won at the price of so much suffering, martyrdom and death; the liberties wrested from his masters after such a bloody struggle, were to make of his life, of the life of the masses, a not too heavy burden to bear.

To this effect, and for this purpose only, was the

Declaration of Independence drafted, the Constitution promulgated, Democracy established, Individualism asserted, Liberalism practised, Freedom defended, Property worshipped.

Alas, to what piteous, mean, corrupted, perverted end have all his efforts for a freer, a better, a fuller life led the common man!

Capitalism in its most hideous form ruling the economic life of the nation; industry serving the machine, not man; great corporations enthroned at the top the social structure gulping all products of the land, all fruits of labor; a few favored individuals enjoying all rights, all liberties, all privileges; the masses deprived of the right to work, the the right to bread, the right to life; a judiciary system become the protector of vested interests; a political system become a mockery and a parody of true democracy; the practice of Individualism degenerated into a shameless struggle for power, for wealth, for prestige; selfishness rampant, destroying all social ties; lust rampant, destroying all life of the spirit.

Truly, to what piteous, mean, corrupted, perverted end have all his efforts for a freer, a better, a fuller life led the common man! What a complete repudiation of America's mission!

It will be no wonder, then, that the common man will awaken finally to the realization that all his liberties avail him nothing, that his rights are trampled upon, denied, destroyed and that to assert them, to realize America's mission in the world, there is one way and one way only: compel wealthy and poor, powerful and weak, governors and governed, to surrender their liberties for the common good, for social security, for the protection of old age, for assistance in the rearing of the family, for the right to toil at the work one enjoys, for the opportunity, finally, to lead the life of a true human being, the opportunity to create through personal effort; because only in the act of creation does man find happiness on this earth, and only through personal contribution to the world's progress can the individual ever hope to be an integral and necessary part of this otherwise utterly strange and decidedly hostile and unintelligible world.

The time is not far distant when the common man will ask himself of what avail are to him his liberties if they cannot protect him against exploition, injustice, sickness and death. Would it not be better for him, is it not imperative for him, that he entrust them to the care of a regime which will protect him and his family, give him back his dignity as a human being, and make of him a necessary part of human society and an integral cell of the moral universe?

A regime, of course, which is only a system of violence, of despotism, of tyranny and force, cannot accomplish, and could never accomplish, such a task.

But these aspects of Fascism are only the transient aspects which accompany it in its first appearance as a political system bidding for recognition, affirmation and power.

There is instead the profound, significant, timeless aspect of Fascism as a way of life, and this aspect America cannot ignore as easily as some people may wish it could.

"Fascism considered as idea, doctrine and philosophy is universal; if it is Italian in its particular institutions, it is universal in its spirit."

These words of the father of Fascism are a confirmation of its dual aspect: the orthodox of tyrannical slavery of bodies and souls of men and the esoteric one of a true philosophy and way of life.

It is under this second aspect that Fascism delivers its message of the type of life that must be lived, if the western world is not to end in utter ruin. This message of Fascism is truly a call to a new life; a call to discard the anachronistic, individualistic purposes for those forms of endeavor which are more in tune with the needs of human life, more in harmony with the spirit of the times.

It is under this form, and only under this form, that Fascism must be thought of as a challenge to America. And a defying challenge it is, whether we choose to admit it or not, and whether we attempt to suppress it or not.

But the question may be asked: "Is not our rugged individualism mainly responsible for our spectacular material achievements? No other people, in fact, has ever accomplished as much as we have in such a short length of time. . . ."

A new land, a whole continent, was offered to us to quench our indomitable thirst for life, for more life. We readily, greedily, took possession of it. We engaged in a desperate struggle against the hostile forces set athwart our path. We have finally conquered the earth beneath, the skies above; the elements all have been made our servants; a virgin and savage land we have transformed into a blossoming garden; through vast deserts we have laid a network of iron rails which hold them subjugated forever; over green pastures we have raised those mighty symphonies of steel and stone which we call our cities; we have set the whole land throbbing with intensive agriculture, with industry, with commerce; a magnificent and powerful empire we have called finally into being, an empire which is both the root and the flower of our rugged individualism. . . . What else could we have done to make our material triumph still greater, still more complete?

Clearly, it is not material achievements that are wanting, it is not the vision of the cities we have built, the rivers we have harnessed, the deserts we have peopled, the monuments we have raised, that can belittle our faith in ourselves and in our present philosophy of life.

Something more is needed, something of an entirely different order than a triumph over the world of nature, something which has to do with our social world, with the world of our fellow men.

To survey this world in its present, tragically miserable state, to witness the ruthless stamping out of all possibilities of a satisfactory life of the majority of our fellow beings, to see the chasm created between those who have and those who have not, a chasm growing always wider and deeper, and darker, to see the gospel of communism make such inroads into the very heart of the most naturally endowed country in the world, means the loss of that faith which only a short while ago seemed to us so everlasting and invincible.

To think of the work that has been done, the struggle which made it possible and, at the same time, of the havoc which it has wrought in other people's lives, leaves us bewildered before our own creations and forced to ask sadly of ourselves: "Cui Bono? What for? Are our gains worth the evil we have spread, the unhappiness we have created, the suffering we have caused?"

What is to be done, then?

Clearly, it is something more than mere academic words that we need to bring us out of this unsatisfactory state of living. We need Action. We need an entirely new, a much more adequate philosophy of life.

We had dedicated ourselves to the worship of individualism, we had made a religion of it, had almost created a god out of its magic power, and lo, the idol of clay has fallen from its high pedestal and lies now at our feet, and we are utterly bewildered and lost. No outlet is left now to us for the expression of our inner powers, used once to their utmost to further our material welfare.

We must find, therefore, not only a new meaning for life, but a purpose must be restored to our efforts; we must, in other words, discover anew the relationship Man-God-Universe, because we have lost our faith in all we once believed and we have no support left for the life of the spirit. This is indeed a crucial time, a critical moment marking a turning point in the history of the western world. All idols destroyed, all beliefs dissolved, all ideals denied, all authorities derided, we stand free of any constraint on our inner life.

Shall we drift hopelessly into an intellectual, moral and spiritual anarchy leading to that final bankruptcy of our civilization anticipated by

Spengler, or will we raise on the deserted altars other idols and worship thus other fallacies; fashion for ourselves new rules of conduct at each new gospel of science, rules which we shall repudiate again tomorrow when we shall find them unable to lead us toward the good life. Or shall we go along living blindly as we are living today, relying on our instincts, our passions, our emotions, when they are driving us toward utter ruin?

Why shall we take any further interest in life when its highest goal: the life of the spirit, is becoming more and more devoid of any meaning, any value?

Are our skyscrapers and our highways, our bridges and our industrial plants, our automobiles and our other machines, all the fruits of our labors, in short, which are poisoning our very life, or, at least, the lives of twenty millions of our brethren, worth more than a single human life?

What is to be done, then?

This we do not know, but what we do know is that we must find a way out of our tragic plight, that we must drink at a new spring of life's force, that we must vivify, transform and spiritualize our dead forms of life if we want to stave off decay.

But it is not only life and more life that matters. What matters is the right conduct of life. What matters is the knowledge of our supreme good and how to realize the good life. What matters is the restoration of our faith in God and the Soul and the fellowship of Man, the supremacy of ideals and the worth of martyrdom, the beauty of heroism and the redemption of sacrifice, the significance of living and the sacredness of death. This is what matters and what has to be taught to us anew.

But to whom shall we appeal for help?

Who will show us the way?

These questions, clamoring for an answer, bring us back to the consideration that an inner necessity must inevitably determine the whole course of human history; that the birth and growth of Fascism, coming as it does at this particular time of stress and strain for western civilization, must be considered, therefore, as a phenomenon of the highest importance for the destiny of mankind.

Because Fascism, in its esoteric aspect, answers a dire need of mankind: the need of starting a new life if salvation is to be found and can be found at all. We must never forget that salvation depends not upon a transformation of the social structure or from a modification of political systems, or from improvements of the economic factors, but from A RADICAL CHANGE OF OUR WHOLE OUTLOOK ON LIFE.

All our attempts to build up a new national economy are bound to end in miserable failure if they are not leavened by a revived spiritual outlook of the problems which beset humanity, as the economical aspects of these problems are ultimately dependent upon the moral ones; are determined by the way in which we solve the age-old struggle between our selfish aims and the claims of our fellow beings and of mankind as a whole.

Such a struggle goes on eternally in the heart of man, but in those dark periods of history characterized by the triumph of individualism it can hardly be called a struggle at all; its outcome being already fore-ordained by the assumptions on which that negative, disintegrating, anti-social philosophy of life is based.

The birth of Fascism could not but intensify this struggle and bring it, for good or bad, to that fatal climax when each individual is faced squarely by the issue whether he chooses to be a truly social being or not, and whether, therefore, he truly deserves the name of man.

We have made of our individual life an end to itself. Let us, from now on, make of it a means to a greater end—the building up of our national life, the building up of our brethren's life. But we have also made of the masses of anonymous, un-articulated beings our "idola fori;" let us, from now on, recognize the worth of the élite of the Spirit, let us acknowledge the need of the aristocracy of the Mind in our midst, let us confess that "Universal History, the history of what man has accomplished in this world, is, at bottom, the History of the Great Men who have worked here." Let us, from now on, give back to our leaders the right and the possibility of leadership, resting satisfied with the role which Nature has assigned to us. We have enthroned Liberty in the market-place and denied it to our inner nature; let us, from now on restore Liberty to what it rightly belongs: to the Spirit of Man; let us think of our duties as moral beings, let us recognize our obligations as social beings, let us allow, in other words, to the Spirit within, freedom to shape the course of our life for the furtherance of higher aims than the satisfaction of senses.

And if to accomplish such purpose we must avail ourselves of the principles of Fascism, what of it? Fascism, with its call of duty to our country, to sacrifice for our fellow beings, to national brotherhood, to belief in God and the human soul, may appear to us as delivering a message at the same time too spiritual and too authoritative to be in tune with our true nature.

But let us remember that nothing great was ever accomplished by the cold, dispassionate calculations of the mind. Only a frenzy of the Spirit can arouse the souls of men from their lethargic slumber and unleash the daemonic forces which can transform and vivify the life of mankind.

THE END